THE CAREER BRAND for PROFESSIONALS

Enhancing Your Brand
Igniting Your Career

LATRICE COLLINS

LATRICE COLLINS

Books by Latrice Collins
The Career Brand for Christians
The Perfect Fit for Careers (e-book)
The Perfect Fit for Careers Journal
The Perfect Fit for Careers Journal: The Companion Guide
Career Planning and Personal Advancement Workbook
Career Planning and Personal Advancement Workbook for Leaders

Workshops and Other Tools by Latrice Collins
Brand Ignition
Brand Impact
Wonderfully Made (Christian Career Branding)
The Career Brand™ Evaluation Tool (www.TheCareerBrand360.com)
Career Brand Small Group Coaching Program

Copyright © 2011, 2014, and 2015 by Latrice Collins.

ISBN: 978-0-9660451-4-7

All rights reserved. No part of this book may be reproduced or transmitted in any form or by any means, electronic or mechanical, including photocopying, recording, or by any information storage and retrieval system, without permission in writing from the copyright owner.

For additional information, contact The Career Brand™ at www.TheCareerBrand.com

This book was created in the United States of America.

LATRICE COLLINS

TABLE OF CONTENTS

Prologue	**7**
Preface	**9**
The Career Brand™	**13**
Introduction to The Career Brand™	13
Analyzing the Life Behind the Brand	**15**
Your Personal Career Journey	16
Journey of Experience	17
Journey of Experience Lessons	18
The Career Brand™	**25**
What is a Brand?	26
The Career Brand™ Model	27
Elements of a Brand	28
Key Element: Expertise	29
Key Element: Image	29
Key Element: Character	29
Key Element: Impact	30
The Career Brand™ Elements and Attributes	31
Attributes of Expertise	32
Attributes of Image	33
Attributes of Character	34
Attributes of Impact	35
The Career Brand™ Evaluation Tool	**37**
Create a Login Account	38
Create Your Profile	38
Complete Your Self-Assessment	38
Invite Others to Evaluate You	38

Reviewing and Analyzing Your Brand Results	**41**
Individual Rating vs. 360-Degree Feedback	43
Feedback	43
Receiving Feedback	45
The Career Brand™ Value	47
Attribute Rating	48
Brand Element Value	49
Overall Brand Value	51
Career-Sabotaging Behaviors (CSB)	52
Strengthening Your Expertise	**55**
Job Knowledge	58
Business Knowledge	60
Work Quality	64
Teachability	65
Credibility	68
Strengthening Your Image	**71**
Interpersonal Skills	73
Service Quality	74
Verbal Communications	75
Appearance	80
Charisma	93
Strengthening Your Character	**95**
Adapting to Change	97
Personal Learning Development	101
Ownership	101
Integrity and Trust	102
Dependability	103

Strengthening Your Impact — 105
- Drive and Perseverance — 107
- Customer Impact/Added Value — 108
- Compliance — 109
- Productivity — 110
- Judgment — 112

Marketing Your Brand — 113
- Marketing Your Brand — 114
- Written Representation — 114
- Personal Representation — 116
- Volunteering Your Brand Strengths — 117
- Brand Application Matrix — 118

What You Need and Want — 121
- Atmosphere for Greatest Potential (AGP) — 123
- Industry — 124
- AGP Pyramid — 127
- Company Culture and Character — 130
- Roles — 133

Networking — 135
- Finding Leads — 139
- Online — 140
- Associations — 140
- Community Events — 141

Winning the Interview — 143
- Types of Interviews — 144
- Screening Interview — 144

Telephone Interview	144
Behavioral (or Situational) Interview	145
Group Interview	145
Informational Interview	146
One-on-One Interview	146
Lunch Interview	146
Skills Interview	147
Stress Interview	147
Creating an Interview Strategy	147
Before the Interview	147
Preparing Your interview Strategy	150
Interview Planning	151
What to Take With You	151
Arrival Time	151
Look the Part	151
Dress Code	151
Salary	152
Setting the Tone	152
What to Leave With	154
After the Interview	154
Questions You May Be Asked	155
Questions You Can Ask the Interviewer	157
Salary Negotiation Tips	158

About the Author — **161**

PROLOGUE

The job market classifies all job openings in two distinct categories: advertised and hidden.

Advertised openings represent jobs that are advertised for the public. Recruiters uses various means to attract potential candidates to the openings such as job fairs, online postings, social media, etc.

The hidden job market represents openings that are NOT advertised. Instead these openings are filled internally or via word of mouth.

Experts estimate 80 percent of all job openings are actually filled through the hidden job market. So why is this important to you?

Many brand programs focus on surface-level brand development, such as how to develop a one-minute (or elevator) speech or how to ensure you are dressed appropriately for the interview. While this is extremely important when you are meeting strangers, this really applies mainly to the 20 percent market.

However, if you are interested in having the highest possibility of success where people come to you with opportunities or

recommends you for an opening, then it's imperative that you focus on your entire career brand.

The Career Brand™ series looks at the holistic approach to your brand. We focus on four elements, 20 attributes, Career-Sabotaging Behaviors and Career-Enhancing Behaviors.

The Career Brand™ books, classes and tools focuses on 68 measurable behaviors to help you:

- Identify the strength of your brand,
- Refine your blind spots and
- Market your brand to position you for the hidden job opportunities.

The beauty of this program is that it uses ALL your experiences and skills to enhance you overall brand value. It doesn't matter what your background is or what type of work you do – EVERYONE should know the value of their own career brand.

PREFACE

I was raised by my mother, who had four daughters and worked two to three jobs while pursuing her college degree. She taught us firsthand the true meaning of strength and tenacity. As you can imagine, there was no room in our house for the word "can't."

After she graduated, she got a job working for a Chicago-based corporation. I used to love watching her get dressed and ready for work. She was simply beautiful. Her hair, clothing, and jewelry were perfect. She was walking elegance with just the right touch of sass.

Well, it took me seven years to complete my undergraduate degree. Like my mom, I worked two to three jobs while attending classes night, day, and on weekends to make it happened.

I remember at one point clearly thinking I was going to lose my mind. Can you imagine my feelings the day I stood among hundreds of other UIC graduates receiving my bachelor's degree? I did it! It was at that moment that I realized I could accomplish anything if I put my mind to it.

Now while I was focused on getting my degree and gaining work experience, I was not so keen on my outer appearance. You know, it is interesting how small things shape your life. For example, I remember at the beginning of my career, someone told me a company in downtown Chicago was hiring. I did not know what the role was or the requirements, I just knew I needed to get dressed and go fill out an application. Truthfully, I did not even know which company it was, so I just went from building to building.

In one particular building, I remember being in the elevator. I had my resume in a portfolio; my suit did not quite fit, and the sleeves were rolled up. My hair was combed but not professionally styled. As I waited in the corner of the elevator (feeling pretty nervous), two women began to look at me and make snide comments about how they hated to see people trying to get a job when they had not bothered to get the split ends clipped from their hair or their sleeves taken up. It was clear they were talking about me. I felt as small as an ant. I surveyed them and the people in the building and realized there was truth to the women's words. If I wanted to get a job in that type of company, I had to tweak a few things about my image in order to be considered for a position.

Over time, I refined my appearance and enhanced my expertise until promotions came quickly. Upon moving to Texas, I acquired a position as a director of HR. At this point in my career, my image was on target, and I had mastered the craft of my profession.

However, one day (to my surprise), I was told I did not quite fit into the culture of the organization because my verbal and writing skills were not up to par. I did not smile enough, my voice was too deep, and I did not seem to have any fear.

I found this offensive and started walking on eggshells to try and be what they wanted. But then, once again, my childhood lessons pushed me forward. My mom would say, "You must be twice as smart and twice as good to be successful." So I told myself, do not get caught in the emotion of the statement; instead, search for the truth. If there is something to enhance, then enhance it; if not, move on.

I was raised in a neighborhood where American Standard English was not commonly used; hence, my articulation of words and use of grammar were not up to the standard of a corporate executive. I therefore worked to refine how I wanted to be seen. I started taking classes, reading books, and acquiring mentors to help me.

In addition, I stopped walking on eggshells and started believing more in my abilities. And guess what – IT ALL WORKED! Leaders began seeking me out to offer me promotions as opposed to me searching for new roles. I had successfully strengthened my personal brand.

It would have been easy to get beaten down by negative comments or missed opportunities and become bitter and frustrated. However, to do that would cheat me out of what life had to offer. Instead, it became important for me to look at myself and identify what I wanted to be and what needed to be refined.

I have been blessed to have accomplished a great deal of success since my early years: I have been an adjunct professor at two accredited colleges, a senior vice president in corporate America, a Toastmaster's president, and a TV talk show host.

Today, I have been on every side of the business table: candidate, HR professional, and business executive. I have coached and developed leaders from churches, government, universities, and corporations. I have changed from being the insecure girl in the elevator to a leader who exudes confidence.

LATRICE COLLINS

A successful career involves knowing yourself and discovering your career brand. In this book, *The Career Brand for Professionals*, I will help you build your personal brand, then identify what you need and want from a company, and finally we will explore strategies for merging the two.

I wish you great success in getting to know and love your unique personal brand, then finding ways to showcase it in a company that will value and appreciate what you bring to the table.

THE CAREER BRAND™ (TCB)

INTRODUCTION TO TCB

Every person is unique with different personalities, experiences, skills and possibilities. In the same light, each company is unique, with different management styles, sizes, and cultures.

The Career Brand™ contains a program that helps you assess both your brand and your company's brand to determine your perfect fit!

Our formula for **The Career Brand™** is simple: evaluate your personal career brand and identify the atmosphere for your greatest potential to pinpoint **The Perfect Fit** just for you.

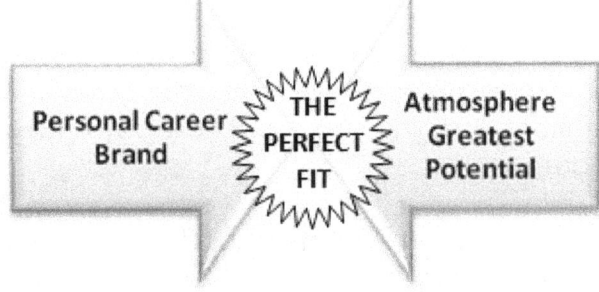

This *Career Brand for Professionals* book is part of **The Career Brand™** Program. This is an *introspective* book filled with thought-provoking questions and templates designed to bring out the very best in you.

This handbook includes significant empowering tools. Upon completing this handbook, you will be able to:

- reflect on your journey of experience
- determine the strengths of your brand
- identify any Career-Sabotaging Behaviors
- assess your brand value
- determine your needs and wants from an employer
- identify your needs and wants from a role
- review nine types of interviews
- review interviewing questions
- develop a salary negotiation strategy

The Career Brand for Professionals is customized to use as a type of introspective journal to help you find your uniqueness. This is not about changing your brand – it is about how to understand and enhance yourself to your full potential.

This small book is designed so it can be reviewed minutes before an important meeting or interview. In other cases, it will serve as your affirmation to remind you of just how powerful and unique you really are.

Are you ready to open your mind and see yourself and your career possibilities from new lenses? Then let us begin your quest to identify your career brand.

LATRICE COLLINS

ANALYZING THE LIFE BEHIND THE BRAND

YOUR PERSONAL CAREER JOURNEY

Throughout a career journey, you'll experience events that are career- and sometimes life-altering. Some of the events are joyous and empowering while others may be sorrowful and sometimes devastating. Before determining your personal career brand, it is important to reflect on your career journey.

Let us take a look at the Journey of Experience diagram on the next page. It is a symbol of your career journey. Each curve on the image depicts an experience that significantly affected either a major career move or an emotional career experience.

Instructions

The lines provided on the Journey of Experience image represent memorable events. Use the lines to write down key life- or career-changing moments.

Think back to significant events that occurred in your career. If the event is either linked to a key emotion or it created a significant change, write it down using a single word or a short phrase that best describes the event. Examples would include "first to graduate college," "first real job," "laid off," or "promoted to manager." If you need additional space, add more lines inside of the image.

JOURNEY OF EXPERIENCE

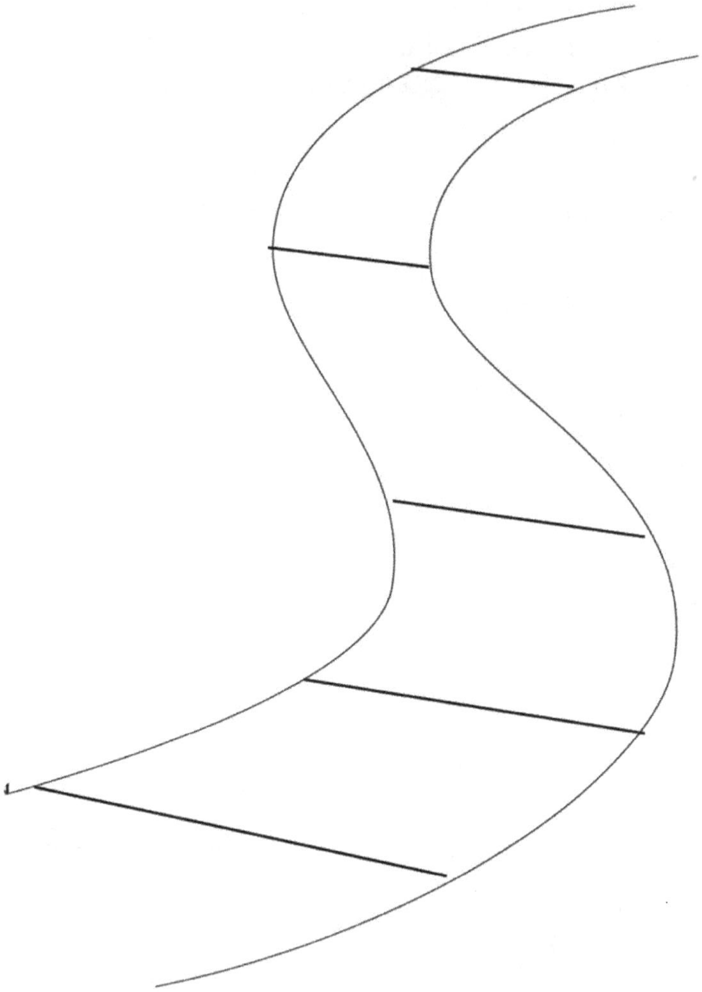

JOURNEY OF EXPERIENCE LESSONS

Now that you have written down your experiences, take a moment to reflect. Review your responses and identify the attributes that you developed as a direct result of those experiences. Check all the boxes that apply. If we missed something, write it in the blank spaces.

- ☐ Has broader understanding
- ☐ Grew as a man/woman
- ☐ Became more open-minded
- ☐ Became a stronger leader
- ☐ Became more independent
- ☐ Began to respect others
- ☐ Became goal-oriented
- ☐ Increased patience
- ☐ Gained stronger character
- ☐ Obtained a stronger family life
- ☐ Became more proficient on the job
- ☐ Expanded my knowledge
- ☐ Became more refined
- ☐ Enhanced my external image
- ☐ Became a better listener
- ☐ Learned to respect others
- ☐ Became more productive
- ☐ Learned to identify risk faster
- ☐ Have never been helped*
- ☐ Have never been rewarded for all the work I do*
- ☐ Since I am not in the "in" crowd I can't get ahead*
- ☐ Jealously from others has kept me from moving up*
- ☐ _____
- ☐ _____

EVERY single situation shapes us in one way or another. Positive experiences provide rewards, which results in individuals increasing their self-worth and/or faith in others. On the other hand, negative experiences (or those we perceive as unfair) hurt. These negative experiences can impact self-esteem. Sometimes the results of these experiences cause individuals to erect walls to protect themselves. Unfortunately, this act also isolates them from others.

This is a good time to reflect and identify if there is one or more career or life lessons you may have missed. Just like in life, there is a lesson in every experience. Every lesson makes a person stronger or wiser. Did you notice some of the statements had a star (*) to the right of them? Review these items closely. A check in one of these boxes may mean you have not learned your life lesson yet.

Here is a hint: if you find you continue to have the same things happening to you repeatedly, there is a great chance that you have not learned the intended lesson.

Take a moment to review your Journey of Experience again. Then answer the questions in the space provided below.

* ITEMS OF THE JOURNEY OF EXPERIENCE LESSONS

If you selected any stars (*) in the Journey of Experience lessons, these are considered opportunities for growth.

There are four steps to analyzing this section.

1. Identify the starred (*) items.
2. Think back to any circumstance(s) that may validate why you feel this way.
3. Answer the question, "Have I contributed to the problem?"
4. Analyze the circumstances to seek out ANY lesson.

SAMPLE ANALYSIS

Checked box	I'm the best but never get rewarded for it.
Circumstances	Two of my peers have been promoted, who produced less than I did.
My Contributions to the Problem	While my production numbers were great, I typically had the lowest quality score and argued often with my team.
Lessons	I need to focus more attention on reducing my errors. Also, I need to work on controlling my temper to keep from isolating my team.

Checked box	
Circumstances	
My Contributions to the Problem	
Lessons	

Reflection

The final step in the Journey of Experience exercise is to summarize your life lessons. Once you can recognize there is value in all experiences, you can move forward to overcoming ANY obstacle.

What did you learn about yourself from the Journey of Experience?

THE CAREER BRAND™

EXPERTISE	IMAGE
CHARACTER	IMPACT

WHAT IS A BRAND?

Before we discuss The Career Brand™, let us first define branding.

What is a brand? Some think it is a logo. Others believe it is a name or a slogan. In truth, a "brand" is far more encompassing than one simple image or slogan.

Background to Branding

In general, the term "branding" represents the entire experience an individual has with a product and/or its company. It is the combination of various touch points that shapes the impression an individual has of that product or company, such as personal experience with the product and advertisement about the product.

Some recognizable brands are Coca-Cola, Mercedes, and Tiffany & Co. Each of these brands is known by its well-publicized, packaged image, such as the red can with the white cursive "Coca-Cola" or the sleek emblem of Mercedes. And who does not recognize the soft greenish-blue Tiffany's box? Each of these companies has created products that catch your eye with their packaging, but they have also established a consistent high quality in their product.

All products have some form of branding. Some are stronger than others. Some have an excellent brand image and some have a poor image.

So how does this apply to you? In the case of **The Career Brand™**, you ARE the product. You are one-of-a-kind, unique from any other individual. This makes you a rare and valuable product.

The Career Brand™ describes the introspective perspective of how you see yourself and the external perspective of how others interpret your behaviors. This means TPF brand helps you to recognize how you see yourself AND how others view you based on the behaviors you demonstrate to them.

Identifying your brand is important in instilling self-value and in elevating yourself to your full potential.

Note there are literally millions of people who are unemployed or underemployed today. In order to obtain the role of your dreams, you have to communicate and demonstrate your best BRAND image to potential employers.

THE CAREER BRAND™ MODEL

Now that we understand what a brand is, the next question is how others see your brand.

An important aspect to a job search, networking, or otherwise developing your career is to first understand what your brand image is.

In this section of *The Career Brand*™, you will

1. Review the four elements of a brand
2. Identify the attributes associated with each element
3. Be introduced to the brand evaluator web-based tool
4. Interpret your personal brand value results

Enhancing your brand can be electrifying. The Career Brand™ Evaluator tool provides a way to introspectively assess your attributes from the company's perspective. Knowing your brand provides you with an opportunity to market yourself and demonstrate to companies how you will represent them.

The Career Brand™ model compiles four key elements into one self-awareness tool. Unlike many of the assessments you have seen on the market, this model asks you a few simple questions about your professional qualities and then assesses the weight of the four elements based on your results. More simply put, we have identified the four elements that are significant to the average employer. The tool will help you rate yourself on each element to identify how employers see you.

ELEMENTS OF A BRAND

The Career Brand™ is comprised of four key elements: expertise, image, character, and impact. Each brand element answers a critical question of an employer. Take a minute to review each of the four categories.

KEY ELEMENT: EXPERTISE

Description: The "expertise" element encompasses your business knowledge, quality of work, and level of work production.

 This element answers the question, "What do you know?"

KEY ELEMENT: IMAGE

Description: The "image" element encompasses your external approachability. This is the element where people form their first impression of you. It is the first level for obtaining credibility from your audience. Examples of image include dress, hair, verbal communication skills, and interpersonal skills.

 This element answers the question, "How will you represent the company?"

KEY ELEMENT: CHARACTER

Description: The "character" element focuses on your personal ethics and values; it also emphasizes your ability to develop, learn, and relate to others.

 This element answers the question, "How do you fit into the company's culture?"

KEY ELEMENT: IMPACT

Description: The "impact" element is a critical element. It identifies how much you cost, save, and generate in terms of funds or output for the organization.

 **This element answers the question, "What will you do for the organization?"**

Managers and interviewers consider these four elements when assessing your value to their organization.

THE CAREER BRAND™ ELEMENTS AND ATTRIBUTES

Each key element is built upon five attributes. The Career Brand™ Evaluation tool measures your Perfect Fit brand image using the twenty attributes listed below.

Expertise	Image
Attributes	Attributes
1. Job knowledge 2. Business knowledge 3. Work quality 4. Teachability 5. Credibility	1. Interpersonal skills 2. Service quality 3. Verbal communication skills 4. Appearance 5. Charisma
Character	**Impact**
Attributes	Attributes
1. Adapting to change 2. Personal learning development 3. Ownership 4. Integrity and trust 5. Dependability	1. Drive and perseverance 2. Customer impact / added value 3. Compliance 4. Productivity 5. Judgment

ATTRIBUTES OF EXPERTISE

1. JOB KNOWLEDGE

Job knowledge refers to the functional and technical skills that measure the ability to do the specific job role and/or function.

2. BUSINESS KNOWLEDGE

Business knowledge measures your understanding of the big picture. It is the sum of how each role connects to the company and how the company makes money, controls expenses, and measures up against the competition.

3. WORK QUALITY

Work quality represents the level of work or service completed with respect to the amount of errors, rework, or efficiencies necessary to meet the work or production standards. A second aspect of work quality includes the level of professionalism or accuracy that you instill into a project, product, or service.

4. TEACHABLILITY

Teachability means you are open and capable of being taught.

5. CREDIBILITY

Credibility describes how believable you are to other people.

ATTRIBUTES OF IMAGE

1. INTERPERSONAL SKILLS

Interpersonal skills are the ability to create an atmosphere where others feel comfortable. This attribute encompasses the ability to relate to and communicate with a range of different individuals.

2. SERVICE QUALITY

Service quality focuses on the quality of care and attention you provide to the customers and/or their specific needs.

3. VERBAL COMMUNICATION SKILLS

Verbal skills assess your ability to communicate using American Standard English and maintain a level of geographical neutrality during business interactions.

4. APPEARANCE

Appearance is the physical image you portray. This includes clothing style, hair, mannerisms, and hygiene.

5. CHARISMA

Charisma is the ability to attract, inspire, and influence people without having any direct authority over them.

ATTRIBUTES OF CHARACTER

1. ADAPTING TO CHANGE

Adapting to change measures the ability to flex to new processes, technology, or standards in the workforce.

2. SELF-DEVELOPMENT

Personal learning competency measures the ability to flex and adapt to your surroundings.

3. OWNERSHIP

Ownership measures the extent to which a person takes on accountability and responsibility for ensuring the work is done.

4. INTEGRITY AND TRUST

This attribute measures whether your words match your actions and whether you are driven by moral and/or ethical principles.

5. DEPENDABILITY

Dependability means being a person who can be counted on.

ATTRIBUTES OF IMPACT

1. DRIVE AND PERSEVERANCE
Perseverance represents dedication to making things happen regardless of obstacles that may be present.

2. CUSTOMER IMPACT/ADDED VALUE

Customer impact and added value focuses on attention and service levels that you provide to internal and external customers.

3. COMPLIANCE

Compliance focuses on the level to which you adhere to the given policies or law.

4. PRODUCTIVITY

Productivity answers the question, "What is the measurable outcome of your work?"

5. JUDGMENT

Judgment defines your ability to make good and sound decisions.

THE CAREER BRAND™ EVALUATION TOOL
(www.TheCareerBrand360.com)

TheCareerBrand360.com is a powerful web-based self-evaluation and 360-degree evaluation tool that uses behavior-based questions to identify your career brand value. It assesses how you see your brand compared to how others see it.

The true power of this tool is that it allows you to see how other people see you! No more guessing and wondering. Wow! Now that is POWERFUL!

The Career Brand™ Evaluation tool is available at a nominal fee online. Just go to TheCareerBrand360.com to get started. The evaluator is easy to use and takes only a few simple steps to activate:

1. Create your profile
2. Complete your self-assessment
3. Invite others to evaluate you
4. Review your personalized career brand comparison report

If you choose not to invest in our Career Brand 360 Evaluation tool today, that's OK. Just remember, feedback is essential to growth, so do your own evaluation. Look for feedback from people you respect. Let them know that you are working on strengthening your career brand and you would value their open feedback.

Here are the four elements and 20 attributes again. Your career brand is built on all 20 attributes.

THE CAREER BRAND™ ELEMENTS AND ATTRIBUTES

Expertise	Image
Attributes	Attributes
1. Job knowledge 2. Business knowledge 3. Work quality 4. Teachability 5. Credibility	1. Interpersonal skills 2. Service quality 3. Verbal communication skills 4. Appearance 5. Charisma |//

Character	Impact
Attributes	Attributes
1. Adapting to change 2. Personal learning development 3. Ownership 4. Integrity and trust 5. Dependability	1. Drive and perseverance 2. Customer impact / added value 3. Compliance 4. Productivity 5. Judgment

IMPORTANT NOTE: Our Career Brand Evaluation tool is built with a feature where all responses are anonymous. This allows reviewers to feel comfortable with providing honest feedback without fear of retaliation. As a result, you receive a clear picture of your brand without any harm to relationships.

If you conduct your own analysis, your responses will either be in person or submitted directly from your reviewer via a phone call or email. Try to make your reviewers feel as comfortable as possible sharing their feedback.

If you are conducting your own evaluation, you may choose to skip the Reviewing and Analyzing Your Brand Results chapter.

REVIEWING AND ANALYZING YOUR BRAND RESULTS

We have covered quite a bit. Hopefully by now you can see yourself from various different perspectives. For some of you, your head may be spinning right about now. But don't fret. Deep-diving into the layers for your brand is like cleaning your closet. YIKES!

At first you think it will take only a quick hour or so to organize it. Then, before you know it, three hours have passed – and your closet, bathroom, and bedroom look like a bomb has exploded in all of them. Does this sound familiar? Then you think, "What happened? What is all this stuff?" You may feel overwhelmed and sorry you started. But you know from experience it will turn out better. Now you just need to decide what you are getting rid of and how to organize what remains.

The same is true for your work here. This chapter is designed to help you understand what you have buried in the closet and work on ways to showcase your strengths more effectively.

Now, let's review your Brand Evaluation report. For holistic results, be sure to invite people you trust to complete the 360- degree brand feedback on you.

Remember, no one is perfect, no not one. So don't get frustrated if your brand results are not perfect. Instead, use your results as an opportunity to grow and not an excuse to start judging the people who provided feedback.

INDIVIDUAL RATING VS. RESPECTED FEEDBACK

FEEDBACK

Feedback is the communications shared from one person to another based on their observation of a particular event. There are two important things to remember about feedback:

It Is a Gift	It May or May Not Be Accurate

• It is typically given because the person cares • You COULD cherish or value it • You DO NOT have to like it • You DO NOT have to accept it	• You SHOULD stop to listen to feedback • Then process it by asking yourself a few questions. • What part of the feedback they are sharing is factual or accurate? How will the feedback benefit me in the short or long term? Is this something I have the power to change or incorporate? What part, if any, should I discard?

It would be wonderful if all feedback was given from a pure heart, but truthfully, some people who give feedback are opinionated, lack values, and do not add any value to your personal growth. Its intent is to HARM you not BUILD you. Therefore, it's important to learn how to weed out the benefits of feedback and how to discard judgmental opinions.

Example: Let's use an example provided earlier.

What to Keep?	What to Discard
Enhance written communication skills. (Why? Because it will help the person grow professionally and personally)	Deep voice and birth origin comment. (Why? Because it is a personal attribute that cannot be changed and it has no value)

RECEIVING FEEDBACK

One the flip side, constructive feedback is extremely valuable. One of the biggest injustices anyone can do to themselves is not obtaining feedback from others.

When we see only from our personal viewpoint, we miss precious opportunities to advance and grow. We see ourselves from the lens of our intentions, (not our behavior). Others judge our brand based on their interpretation of our actual behavior. Together we can obtain a panoramic view of our actions that shape our brand.

During the time when I was a talk show host, after one show an audience member described the difficulties of landing a job. As he spoke, he was oblivious to the fact that he came across very angry, hurt, and frustrated; no matter what we said, he quickly rejected the feedback and assured everyone that was NOT how he operated in general.

What do you think? Do you think the essence of his frustration seeped out during job interviews? Do you think this person saw themselves with a clear lens?

Here are a few important tips when reviewing your results:

1. Review your feedback results carefully.
2. Compare each result with your self-evaluation.
3. Identify where you have similarities.
4. Identify where you have gaps.
5. Identify where you rate yourself higher.
6. Identify where they rated you higher.
7. Formulate your strategy for refining your growth opportunities.
8. Formulate your strategy for marketing your strengths.

THE CAREER BRAND™ VALUE

As we stated before, The Career Brand™ is built on the four key elements: Expertise, Image, Character and Impact. As part of your evaluation, your work behavior was assessed based on 20 attributes that which linked to the four elements.

The evaluation tool uses a formula to assess three levels of your Career Brand value:

1. Your Attribute Skill Level
2. Your Brand Element Value
3. Your Overall Career Brand Value

Sample Chart

THE CAREER BRAND MODEL

Overall Career Brand Value

BRAND ELEMENT "Expertise"	BRAND ELEMENT "Image"	BRAND ELEMENT "Character"	BRAND ELEMENT "Impact"
ATTRIBUTES	**ATTRIBUTES**	**ATTRIBUTES**	**ATTRIBUTES**
Job Knowledge	Interpersonal Skills	Adapting to Change	Drive and Perseverance
Business Knowledge	Service Quality	Self Development	Customer Impact /
Work Quality	Verbal Communication Skills	Ownership Integrity and Trust	Added Value
Teachable	Appearance	Dependability	Compliance
Credibility	Charisma		Productivity Judgment

ATTRIBUTE RATING
LEVEL 1

Attributes refer to your knowledge, skills and/or behaviors. Attributes are typically behaviors people can observe, such as something they can see, hear, read, or smell.

The evaluation tool uses observable scenarios (not ratings) to determine your brand value. For instance, some surveys ask you to rate yourself on a one-to-five scale to determine your value; however, that can be very subjective. The Career Brand™ Evaluation tool uses a behavior questionnaire to assess how people see you based on your own behavior, not a subjective sliding scale.

The brand attribute rating communicates the level of skill you have demonstrated in each of the 20 attributes. The answers provided through the assessment are then calculated to determine each attribute's skill level. There are three skill levels.

Attribute Skill Level	Demonstrated Skill
Expert	Role Model of Excellence
Skilled	Proficient and Self-Sufficient
Under-skilled	Requires Additional Refinement

BRAND ELEMENT VALUE
LEVEL 2

Level 2 of the brand value is the Brand Element value. The Brand Element value is a rollup of your brand attributes and your Career-Sabotaging Behaviors (CSB). We will talk about those a little later.

These ratings are combined and calculated to illustrate the strength of each element value. These results can also be helpful with identifying potential blind spots that may negatively influence your career growth.

There are three Brand Element values:

TOP PERFORMER:

An individual with an element rated as TOP PERFORMER represents a person who DEMONSTRATES attributes that are mostly rated as Expert. Individuals in this classification are usually within the top 15 percent of all individuals surveyed.

PERFORMER:

An individual with an element rated as PERFORMER represents a person who DEMONSTRATES attributes with a range of skill sets. These ratings can expand across all three skill levels: Under-skilled, Skilled, and Expert. However, the consolidated weighting indicates the person would perform reasonably for the organization.

UNRECOGNIZED POTENTIAL

An individual with an element rated as UNRECOGNIZED POTENTIAL represents a person who has NOT DEMONSTRATED the skills in a manner that is positively recognizable by the reviewers. In this case, an element has at least three of the five attributes coded as Under-skilled.

Note: Being rated UNRECOGNIZED POTENTIAL does not mean the person does not possess skills; it simply means the strength of the person have not been adequately demonstrated through the behaviors that have been presented to and observed by the reviewers.

OVERALL CAREER BRAND VALUE
LEVEL 3

The Career Brand™ Evaluation tool assesses your combined element ratings and CSB to determine your overall brand values. Remember, hiring managers determine who to hire in a position based on the answers to four questions:

- Expertise: What do you know?
- Image: How will you represent our company?
- Character: How will you fit with our company?
- Impact: What will you do for our company?

Individuals whose responses provide the best fit to the aforementioned questions typically escalate to the final selection pool for the position being sought. The overall brand values can fall into one of five levels:

1. Exceptional Career Brand
2. Superior Career Brand
3. Satisfactory Career Brand
4. Moderately Satisfactory Career Brand
5. Unsatisfactory Career Brand

In many cases, Levels 1 through 4 are sufficient to gain employment (depending on the type of work you are seeking). However, the higher you wish to climb, the more important it becomes to strengthen your brand rating to beat out the competition.

CAREER-SABOTAGING BEHAVIORS (CSB)

After working with thousands of individuals over the years, I've found it is apparent that sometimes WE are our worst enemies. What do I mean by that?

Sometimes we have mastered each attribute and element, creating what would be a very strong brand. However, because of varying idiosyncrasies, we exhibit behaviors that become more self-destructive than career-enhancing. Hence, they are sabotaging to our career.

Have you ever met someone and without a doubt they are the smartest or the best at what they do but, they are SOOOOO irritating that you absolutely don't want to work with them or even ask them a question?

We call these behaviors "Career-Sabotaging Behaviors" or CSBs. While that person may at first have rated high on job knowledge for instance, their constant know-it-all attitude decreased their element rating. You might ask, "Why?" Remember the Expertise element answers the question, "What do you know?" That is important because the person they hire can help the company bridge a gap in that section. However, if no one is willing to interact with that person, the gap does not get filled and significant information is never shared with them or learned from them. Eventually, they become a cost, (not an investment), to the company.

The greater the CSB, the stronger the negative impact will be on the brand.

When reviewing your CSB sections, you are looking for two types of patterns:

Do you have a high number of CSBs under one element?
Do you have several people stating you have the same CSB?

For example:
Let's say five people provided feedback.

One person listed one CSB under Expertise. This is not a big deal because it's not a pattern. However, if three out of five people select the same CSB, that is something to focus on because it is an indication that you are consistent with that particular behavior.

If you have a number of responses by numerous people under one element, pay close attention and identify that element as one you want to focus on in the future.

If you have a significant number of CSBs, your brand may be negatively affected.

One important note to remember is that personal strengths used in excess can be viewed as weaknesses. Most CSBs are overused strengths (or character traits) that can be minimized by simply decreasing the use of that behavior.

LATRICE COLLINS

STRENGTHENING YOUR EXPERTISE

The next four chapters of this handbook are designed as a plug-and-play. You can select the chapters or sections that are most applicable to your needs.

For example, if you were rated a "preferred choice" under the Expertise element, feel free to skip this chapter and go directly to Image. However, if your Business Knowledge attribute under the Expertise element was rated as under-skilled, you may want to take a moment to review those pages of the chapter.

THE EXPERTISE ELEMENT ANSWERS THE QUESTION, WHAT DO YOU KNOW?

Individuals with high levels under Expertise become the go-to resource. Maybe you want to be the person your boss seeks out when he/she needs answers. This is the element where enhancing your knowledge and/or refining your work quality can elevate you to an expert in the minds of others.

This is typically the strongest brand element for people who have been working for several years in the same field. For now, let's deep-dive into the attributes linked to this element.

Image
Attributes
1. Job knowledge 2. Business knowledge 3. Work quality 4. Teachability 5. Credibility

JOB KNOWLEDGE

The Job Knowledge attribute denotes the skill you demonstrate in understanding your specific role. Whether your role is that of a teacher, a project manager, a housekeeper, or a corporate executive, this attribute communicates how well you know your job.

There are many ways to improve your job knowledge. Methods will range depending on whether you work in a company that has several people in the same role or if your role is unique and different from others.

Here are a few steps for building your job knowledge while improving the impression others have for you in this attribute:

1. Work to understand how your role impacts the team and the company.
2. Identify the expectations of your manager, clients (internal and external), and/or teammates. It is important to understand what the picture of success looks like in the eyes of each individual or group you are helping. For instance, your clients may consider you knowledgeable if you can answer their questions quickly and in plain English, while your teammates only consider you knowledgeable if you can perform tasks without asking a lot of questions.
3. Of the items listed in Step 2, identify the most important information to know and to what extent or depth you need to know it.

4. Review any policy or procedural guideline that may provide a clear walk-through of your responsibilities. If you need to rev up quickly to the current standards, make sure you study on your off-time. Try creating games with a good friend to help you remember laws, rules, and processes.
5. Partner with a strong performer in the company in the area you are weakest. Note: This may require multiple partnerships. Some colleagues may be strong in one area while someone else may be strong in another.
6. IMPORTANT: While you are collecting knowledge from team members, make sure to find ways you can add value back to them. You do not want to become a burden to others or become known as the person who asks everyone for help. You would rather be known as a great team player who helps others and who others feel good about helping as well.
7. If you are in a unique role at your company, and there are no policies, procedures, or people to help you enhance your skill level, try the list below to enhance your skills:
    a. Look into professional associations for tips of the trade.
    b. Check the Internet for quick tips, templates, or guides on the topics you need to learn. Many times there are simple PDFs that someone created that are just the answer you are looking for.
    c. Find one or more mentors who may be willing to assist you in building your job knowledge.

8. Seeing is believing. Look for low-hanging fruit. Don't broadcast with words. Show them. Ask, "What are the top items or most pressing needs?" then try to implement the items that can be completed quickly. Often-times it is easy tasks that are done well and on time that build your reputation the fastest.
9. Apply what you learn and create actionable results. The more you can independently demonstrate your understanding of the job, the greater the impression you will build toward being an expert in this attribute.

BUSINESS KNOWLEDGE

The Business Knowledge attribute denotes your understanding of the company and its industry and a clear understanding of what it takes to run the business effectively.

An individual who is classified as an expert in Business Knowledge has proven he/she understands the inner workings of a company and of its industry.

This attribute is divided into two parts: company knowledge and industry knowledge.

COMPANY KNOWLEDGE

Individuals who are considered experts in company knowledge have a keen ability to identify ways to strengthen the company's business. Their actions are focused on four components that build the company:

1. **Revenue:** How can they increase income from the company's products or services?
2. **Cost control:** How can they control expenses and improve efficiencies?
3. **Customer satisfaction:** How do they create high satisfaction within their customers? By doing so they increase customer loyalty, which transfers into repeat business and referrals. This can be achieved through all forms of communications (or touch points) with the customer.
4. **Quality control:** What checks and balance processes do they have in place to ensure efficiencies and reduce errors so the company operates within the confines of the ethics, policies, or laws that govern it?

To strengthen business knowledge, dissect the company. Get a clear understanding of how the major departments (or functions or divisions) work together. If they are not working together, what are ways they can work together to make the company stronger? You MUST understand each part before you can make recommendations; otherwise, people will become frustrated with you recommending solutions that will not work. Ask yourself the following:

- Which departments/functions contribute to revenue (e.g., sales, marketing, etc.)?

- Which departments/functions monitor quality (legal, compliance, HR, quality control)?
- Which departments/functions connect with your customers (customer service, sales, collections, etc.)?
- Which departments/functions monitor cost control (accounting, engineering, technology, etc.)? Sometimes it is the everyday individual who thinks of ideas to help the company save money.

Once the company is dissected, identify how each department links together to strengthen the company.

See if you can possibly participate in a type of stretch assignment where you work-share to learn other parts of the business. That could have significant impact on expanding your company knowledge.

INDUSTRY KNOWLEDGE

A strong business leader (or manager) is intimately familiar with his/her company and how it compares to similar companies in its industry. Progressive leaders also know their competitors and know how they differ from their company.

To find out more about your industry, search the Internet for associations, networking groups, magazines, and blogs that focus on your specific industry. Industry refers to the category your company falls into such as finance, auto, fast food, or hotel. You might also look at the industry from the perspective of the role you are in, such as management, sales, or operations.

Once you learn more about the industry, such as new trends,

ideas, or risks, focus next on how your company compares to its competitors.

You can identify your company's competitors in a variety of ways:

1. Search the immediate area for establishments that provide the same or similar products or services that you provide.
2. Complete an Internet search on establishments that provide the same or similar products or services that you provide.
3. Search Hoover's. This company is noted for providing detailed information on nearly any company. If you are short on funds for their membership, check your local library for free usage.
4. Finally, if you are a leader of the organization, you can use your industry knowledge to help you differentiate how you want to set your company apart from the competitors. What will be the thing your company is known for that the others don't have?

WORK QUALITY

All the knowledge in the world will not matter one bit if you are known for poor quality and errors. Of the five attributes in the Expertise element, Work Quality is the one that could be the most damaging to your brand.

This is also the hardest to repair, so pay close attention in ensuring to maintain at least a "skilled" impression regarding your attention to detail.

If this is an area that you would like to improve, here are a few helpful tips:

1. Make sure you thoroughly understand all aspects of the job and how each component is measured.
2. Study items you are shaky on. *If there is a helpful book or policy to study, then do so. If not, ask someone who knows the process for help.*
3. Slow down. Most errors occur because of rushing. Give yourself time to recheck your work at a later time or date.
4. Check your work against a checklist. If there is not one available, create one.
5. Ask a peer to help check your work.
6. Once you have proven your checklist works for you, share it with your team members. This can help improve the overall quality of the team while increasing your brand image for this attribute.

TEACHABILITY

As long as there is life left in your body, there is the capacity to learn. Individuals with an Expert level of Teachability have demonstrated a willingness to learn, and they have a willingness to change.

If this is a low-scoring attribute, it would mean others may view you as having either a low willingness to change or a low interest in LISTENING and learning.

A low level of Teachability is a high risk to an organization. Companies are changing rapidly and need to trust that you are moving in the direction of the company. Often-times, people who are low in this attributes are willing to learn; however, they do not understand a few important items:

1. What is the big picture the company or person is trying to explain?
2. What is the impact to you or something you value?
3. How will the change be implemented?

Sometimes striving to obtain answers to one or all of the aforementioned questions creates the perception of pushing back and unwillingness to learn. Your challenge is to create a strategy for discovering answers while demonstrating that you are listening to what they are saying.

Here are a few frank tips to incorporate into your style:

STEP 1: Listen & think big.
Listen closely to identify the big picture and what benefit it is targeted to create. Most changes will have a shortterm or long-term fix. Try to see from their eyes the type of fix the change is designed to create.

STEP 2: Be like Mikey. Try it. You might like it.
Many years ago, Life cereal created a commercial where two boys were afraid of trying the new cereal. They passed the bowl from one another then finally decided to push it off to the toddler, Mikey, to try. Mikey never liked anything. However, Mikey tasted the cereal and loved it. The shocked young boys said, "Hey, Mikey! He likes it!" The slogan became a household expression that reminded people to try things even if they thought they would not like it. So the lesson of the day: Be like Mikey.

1. Take a chance, and try what has been proposed by someone else.
2. Try something new, regardless of whether you think it will or will not work.
3. Identify at least three benefits or positive outcomes of what you've learned. You will be surprised how many things you begin to learn and enjoy.
4. If everything you've learned about somebody else or their ideas is negative, you clearly have NOT learned the entire lesson.

Personal Barriers to Avoid

Individuals who are labeled as "not teachable" may sometime be the same as a person viewed as a know-it-all.

There are two offenders who have this attribute.

1. Those who point out problems, but do not contribute to solutions.
2. Those who do not allow others to contribute to solutions.

If you have been described in this manner, consider the following tips:

- When you are about to disagree because you already know something, STOP. Listen and take notes.
- When you are about to interrupt someone who is telling you how to do something, STOP. Listen and take notes.
- When you are going to state something will not work BEFORE you have listened to everything the person is trying to say, you guessed it, STOP. Listen and take notes.
- Challenge yourself to discover the positives linked to what has been said. This is necessary to grasp a clearer understanding of how other people think.
- Use the Brainstorming and Impact Analysis Form found on our Community Site to help open your mind to something you may have missed.

Two important things to remember:

1. You are not ALWAYS right about EVERYTHING.
2. You CAN learn something important from every person and every situation.

CREDIBILITY

The final attribute under the Expertise element is Credibility. An individual with low levels of Credibility has a difficult time proving the depth of their strength in the other four attributes under Expertise.

One of three factors can cause a loss of credibility:

1. You may not have the in-depth knowledge required to speak on a topic.
2. Your image distracts from your expertise.
3. Past experiences others have had with you diminished trust between you and the individuals you need to influence. This could have occurred from misstatement of facts, not delivering results, or not delivering what was expected.

Any or all of these three items have the ability to crush your brand. Credibility is built on two features: expertise and empathy.

- Expertise encompasses the degree to which you know your subject matter. Those around you must feel that you have dependable, adequate and/or

superior knowledge of the subject at hand.
- With empathy, the others MUST feel you can relate to their circumstances in some way, either as the solution to their problem or because of personal knowledge of their scenario.

A clear example of credibility is demonstrated every election year. Voters must decide which candidate to elect into office. The candidates, who can demonstrate they have expertise in the job and empathize with the constituents have the best chance of winning the election.

Your job is two-fold:

1. Make sure you are accurate in what you say, and it is believable when you say it.
2. Make sure you understand the needs of the individuals you are speaking to and communicate directly to their points of interest.

LATRICE COLLINS

STRENGTHENING YOUR IMAGE

THE IMAGE ELEMENT ANSWERS THE QUESTION, HOW WILL YOU REPRESENT THE COMPANY?

Image is the unspoken eliminator. Most people are unwilling to say you are not promotable because your image is not up to par. But they will show you in multiple ways by NOT elevating you to the level your expertise, character, and impact deserves. So if you want to give your image a face-lift, study and incorporate this section immediately.

Image is the brand element that can remove you from being an option before you have a chance to say a word.

Image
Attributes
1. Interpersonal skills
2. Service quality
3. Verbal communication skills
4. Appearance
5. Charisma

INTERPERSONAL SKILLS

Interpersonal skill is an ability to help other people feel comfortable. For those with the gift of Helping, this is a particularly natural skill. However, developing interpersonal skills can be difficult when this is outside of your normal behavior. This attribute is particularly difficult because different people and cultures look for different behaviors to feel included and welcome.

Stephen Covey said it best in his book, *The 7 Habits of Highly Effective People*. In it he stated, "First seek to understand then to be understood." Individuals who master understanding others have a stronger propensity to master interpersonal skills. Why, you might ask? Because people want to know they are heard and understood. Once they believe they have been heard, they are more willing to also listen to and be comfortable with you.

There are many psychological assessments that help in understanding people more effectively, such as Myers–Briggs and the Jung Career Indicator. Study a variety of these types of tools to help understand the viewpoints of others. You may even learn quite a bit about yourself.

SERVICE QUALITY

There is ONE surefire way to improve service quality for a customer: LISTEN. This is sometimes the simplest and most underutilized skill we can demonstrate.

People (whether it is a peer, customer, church member, a spouse, a child, you name it) want to be cared for. Service is about listening closely to what the individual is requesting and responding <u>appropriately to their needs.</u>

To ensure you understand the needs of other individuals, summarize or paraphrase what they said. If you are correct, they will appreciate that you listened carefully. If you are not correct, apologize and ask them to help clarify the areas you misunderstood.

In most cases, service quality can be improved when you are able to effectively reiterate what the other person is seeking, then empathically and professionally provide a solution (or explanation) of how you can service them.

Note: You may not be able to provide a solution for what they need. When you cannot, provide a recommendation of one or more alternatives. The fact that you listened and understood them provides an added level of comfort to them.

VERBAL COMMUNICATIONS

Think about what happens when you hear someone speak. The clearer their voice and their ability to pronounce their words, the more credible they seem.

On the other hand, when they use poor grammar, the wrong words, or mispronounce words, there is a different impression of them entirely. Have you assessed your verbal communication skills? Remember, your verbal communication skill is different than your comfort in public speaking. There are countless politicians, ministers, teachers, etc. that are comfortable speaking in front of a group; however, their ability to use American Standard English (ASE) is questionable.

Lisa Delpit wrote an intriguing book called *The Skin We Speak*. In it, she described a real-life story of a phenomenal woman who became so great in her field that she was one of only SIX people in the country who could perform a very specific and highly coveted task. Her reputation preceded her in her industry, and she was held in the highest regard. One company was in desperate need of her expertise. They sought her out to come and work on their project. However, upon her meeting the board, they were dismayed at her lack of mastery of verbal communication skills.

She was challenged with word pronunciation and verb usage. They became so bothered by her lack of communication skills that they began to question her knowledge. She eventually lost

credibility and her contract was terminated. While the company representing the woman tried desperately to validate her knowledge level, the hiring company refused to believe thatsomeone who lacked solid speaking skills could possess the knowledge necessary to do the complex job. Of course this is preposterous. She was clearly exceptional in her craft; however, that was only one element. In this case, her Career Brand would have shown a high degree of Expertise and Impact, but a lower value when it came to Image.

The *Perfect Fit for Careers Journal* lists a few examples for testing your speaking ability. However, if you don't have that manual, try this.

EXERCISE

Record yourself while reading an article aloud. Next, carefully listen for certain sounds and enunciation patterns.

There are numerous patterns you may hear, depending on your background or geographical upbringing.

Here are a few common missteps.

The first is the pronunciation of the TH sound. Listen closely at the beginning or the end of a word. Does your pronunciation sound like a D, T, or F instead of the TH sound? If so, verbal communication is something you may want to refine.

In researching this topic it was mind-blowing to identify the extent of the language gap. Such gaps are typically a result of where you grew up more than anything else. So many people face speaking challenges as a result of how they have heard common words. In many cases, it is not that the word is pronounced wrong as much as it is demographically or geographically different.

In those cases sounds and pronunciations are reinforced at home, in school, and around the neighborhood. Now as an adult it is much more difficult to tweak the speaking habits.

Here are a couple of common disconnects.

- Grammatical Noun-Verb Agreement Errors

    She HAVE two pennies instead of she HAS two pennies.

- Dropping the Ends of Words

    I'm *goin* to the house instead of I'm *going* to the house.

In my studies and opportunities to coach and develop individuals, language became one of the hardest areas to coach. There are limited books on the topic that help define patterns of speech based on demographic and geographical patterns.

The only book I have been able to find that is directly related to this topic is called *Speaking Clearly: Improving Voice and Diction*. One of the contributing authors is Jeffrey Hahner. The newest addition comes with a pronunciation CD-ROM.

Various colleges also have writing courses. Some have APA writing courses. These courses are designed to be extremely strict on writing and grammar and can help you immensely with speaking and writing more effectively.

If you are interested in improving in this area, it will require dedication, patience and energy.

So it is time to go back to the basics.

Fine-tune your ear to identify your speech habits. Here are a few suggestions.

- Record yourself whenever possible.
- One VERY inexpensive lesson is Hooked on Phonics. The area you want to focus on should determine which level you should use. The program costs about $30, but it provides great lessons on pronunciation. Keep the cards in the armrest in your vehicle. Take 5 to 15 minutes a day to drive to a quiet, private place and go over the lessons.
- Join a Toastmasters club. Toastmasters is designed to help correct individuals on common speaking challenges. Note: Visit a few clubs to make sure you choose the one best for you. Some clubs are stronger than others. Have a clear understanding of what you are looking for from the club and identify if that club is strong in that area.
- Take an English class at a community college. Oftentimes the challenge with grammar is the lack

of knowing what is correct. Additionally, the rules have changed over the past twenty years; refresher courses are helpful.
- Hire a pathologist or speaking coach. This is the most expensive option; however, it is extremely effective since it is tailored to your specific needs.

APPEARANCE

We live in a visual world where you are sized up based on your physical appearance. The unfortunate truth is you could be the very best at what you do in your field, -but if the first visible impression to an employer is different than their expectation, it is extremely likely (unless you absolutely blow them out the water in every other category) you will not get the job.

Now, there are some hiring managers who are openminded enough to look at experience and impact and ignore appearance. But that type of hiring manager is few and far between or he works in a company that values creativity and individuality over conformity. Again, this is few and far between.

More frequently, individuals are repeatedly discounted and dismissed because they do not meet the image of what an employer is seeking. To ensure you are not removed from the running before you can effectively communicate your brand, this chapter will focus on small ways of improving your personal image.

Because people are visual AND impressions are formed at first glance, we will spend quite a bit of time covering various details of polishing your external appearance. Remember, your appearance is the unspoken message you portray to another individual.

As you walk around every day, you and other individuals are making quick judgments about people solely based on appearance.

This is a section of contention. Many people believe they should be able to dress and wear their hair to their taste and not flex to that of an employer. As long as they do their work, why should it matter? This is very understandable because for many people, their hair and clothing defines their individuality.

The one thing to consider is that every company has its own culture. That culture defines who they are and what their brand image is.

Since the majority of businesses (large and small) are a bit more traditional, this section is written from a more conservative perspective. However, companies' dress attires often vary.

Hair and fashion may be a deal-breaker for you. Some companies are very open-minded and encourage individual expression while other companies are much more conservative.

In reality, the more you demonstrate excellence, the greater the opportunity to show your individuality. At that point, you have demonstrated the essence of your value to their organization and that typically weighs heavier than some of the general standards.

Now let us look at appearance in greater detail.

HAIR

- Your hair should appear neat and healthy. Hair with noticeable sheen will look healthier and speak to the level of care the man or woman gives to his or her grooming. This is significantly more important if you would like to be considered for higher-level positions.

- Split ends should be clipped. Ladies, split ends are not the same as long hair. It signifies damaged hair and distracts from your natural beauty.
- Hairlines should be trimmed neatly.
- Facial hair should be trimmed neatly. This includes eyebrows, upper lips, mustaches, and beards.

If you are in the arts, entertainment, or advertising fields, more extravagant hairstyles may be more acceptable.

Make sure you check out the company culture to confirm.

SKIN

- You skin should be naturally smooth, understanding some people have skin conditions.
- Because of dead skin cell buildup, it is helpful to many people to use a facial scrub to remove dead skin and a toner to cleanse the pores. (There are numerous home remedies found on the Internet if funds are too tight to afford a skin care daily cleansing system.)
- Drink plenty of water and eat vegetables to help your skin glow from the inside out.
- Use a moisturizer (with sunscreen) on your face.
- Use lotion on your hands to ensure your hands are not rough when you shake hands at the interview. Cuticle creams are wonderful for keeping your nail cuticles soft and healthy.
- Cocoa butter lotion used daily helps create an even skin tone.
- Check with your doctor about what is best for you.

FALSE NAILS

- Nails should be low to medium length.
- The safest option is natural and French-cut nails.
- Avoid long false nails; this causes questions around hygiene and the ability to work quickly.

MAKEUP

- There are three levels of makeup application: day wear, night wear, and visual broadcasting.
    - Day wear provides a very natural look. It is meant to accentuate your natural beauty. Day wear consists of light weight foundation, eye liner and/or mild shadows, and lipstick or lip gloss. If blush is worn, it should be in moderation.
    - Evening wear is much more dramatic. It is applied to draw attention by bringing out the smoky eyes, high cheek bones, and luscious lips.
    - Visual broadcasting makeup is a heavy application of foundation, eye lashes, etc., that is applied much thicker because the lights of the camera overpower and flush out standard makeup.

Note: In various parts of the country, heavier makeup is more of an acceptable practice. So know your audience and environment to identify what is the most appropriate for your area.

CLOTHING

Unisex

- Suit jacket sleeves should hit a little past the wrist bone at the base of the hand. (The exception is a women's jacket that is intentionally made to be a shorter sleeve).

- Clothes should be clean and free from odor and wrinkles.

- The style should be appropriate for the company culture and one level above the role you are seeking. *For example, in general it would be inappropriate to wear a suit to an interview for a construction position.*

- Clothes should fit your size. If you are sitting and feel the closure of your pant or skirt cutting into your midsection, the outfit is probably too small.

- If you cannot touch your elbow because a jacket is too constricting, the jacket is too small.

- Socks should match the pant color (this is especially helpful if the pants are a bit too short). To check to make sure your pants are not too short, put on a pair of white socks and your shoes and walk around. If you can clearly see your white socks, the pants are too short.

MEN

- Traditional guideline for the relationship between a suit jacket and the shirt worn under it — about half an inch of the shirt cuff should be visible beyond the jacket cuff.
- As a guideline (not a hard core rule) the shirt sleeve should peek out the sleeve — the seam where the shirt cuff joins the shirt sleeve should never be visible
- The jacket sleeve should never hide the shirt sleeve entirely. At least a small band of shirt cuff should always be visible.
- The pant cuff should rest on the top of your shoe — there needs to be contact, but it shouldn't be more than that. The pant can fall a touch longer in the back than in front, so long as it's still above the heel of the shoe (the actual heel, not just the back of the shoe).

SHOES AND SKIN

- Make sure your shoes are polished and clean.
- The rule on open or closed-toe shoes is based on the company and on the amount of bare skin already showing with your outfit. For example, if a woman is wearing a pant suit, an open-toe shoe is typically acceptable. However, if she is wearing a relatively short skirt and sleeveless top (it gets REALLY HOT in Texas), then she would probably wear a closed-toe shoe as an open-toe shoe would look more like she's going out rather than going to work.

IT NEEDS TO BE SAID

This section lists various items that everyone talks about, but no one says. It may make you a little uncomfortable, but it is needed information.

Sneak Peek Check

Sometimes when people are walking down the street, if one person finds the other one attractive, he or she waits until the person passes then they turn around to take a last sneak peek of them. Ladies, try your sneak peek at home. Before you leave, stand with your back to a fulllength mirror, take one step forward, then turn around and look at yourself in the mirror. If you can see the undergarments you are wearing, you need to change.

Panty lines and bra straps should never show. Today, there are various types of underwear to ensure nothing shows beneath your outfit. There are even clips to help keep straps in place.

Undergarments

I know, I know. You're shaking your head at the picture. But who amongst us have not seen this picture and NOBODY tells the person it is just wrong. The only conclusion is nobody told her the depth of how bad this is or why it's inappropriate. In reality, only someone extremely close to you should have any idea what you are wearing underneath

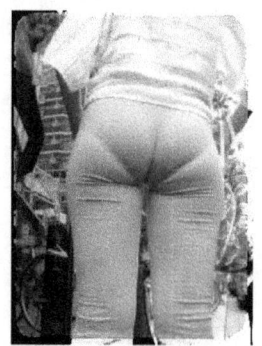

your attire. Today's fashion industry has created an abundance of different types of foundation and lingerie pieces to complement a woman's style and her best assets.

There are numerous types of panties to complement your style: thongs, briefs, boy shorts, high cut, bikini panties etc. Different types are made for different shapes and outfits.

For example, thongs should be worn to keep from seeing panty lines. However, if the thong is TOO small it defeats the purpose. It will show the imprint.

Spanks and/or panty hose can be worn to hold everything in place to keep a polished look. Panty hose are also available with a cotton crotch or with the feet out to allow the body to breath.

> **VISUALIZE**
>
> Ladies, consider your combination of attire. Imagine seeing a woman walk by in an office building. She is wearing a sleeveless fitted blouse, tight very short skirt, no panty hose, and sling back (or strapless) open-toe shoes. What position would you believe she now holds? What position does she not hold? Again, there is no way of knowing; however, judgment calls are made simply by the amount of skin showing or the closeness of the outfit.

LATRICE COLLINS

Take a look at the next page and see if you have a perception about each person based on her attire?

EXERCISE-WOMEN

It's important to remember, different companies have different cultures. What is the standard in one company may not be acceptable in another. Take a look at each person below. Ask yourself the basic questions about each person.

- Where does she work?
- What type of work does she do?
- What is her title?
- What message is she conveying about her brand?

After reviewing each picture, consider your fashion style, your career choice and company preference, and ask yourself how you want to be viewed.

LATRICE COLLINS

EXERCISE-MEN

It's important to remember, different companies have different cultures. What is the standard in one company may not be acceptable in another. Take a look at each person below. Ask yourself the basic questions about each person.

- Where does he work?
- What type of work does he do?
- What is his title?
- What message is he conveying about his brand?

After reviewing each picture, consider your fashion style, your career choice and company preference, and ask yourself how you want to be viewed.

Dress Code Take-Away

While this book is not intended to force you into any one fashion style, I do want you to consider your style as it compares to the company you choose to work for. Then ask yourself, is it a clash or complement? You don't have to always fit exactly with a company; however, the more you do not connect on one level, the more important it is to excel in another.

Hygiene

- Clip nose and ear hairs.

- Ask your doctor about how to clip hair coming out of moles.

- Ladies, shave the hair from under your arms, especially if you want to wear a sleeveless blouse.

- Shave or pluck lip, chin and eye bros

- Make sure body fragrances are not overbearing. Many people are allergic to cologne smells.

- Use deodorant.

- Take a breath mint before the meeting.

- Bathe.

PERSONAL ETIQUETTE AND POLISH

Shaking hands

- Hand shaking is still an important technique that is used to identify the strength of a person. Right hands are used to shake hands. Hands should link at the thumb's crest and grip the other person's entire palm. The grip should be firm but not crushing.
- Shaking hands using the tips of the hand or fingers conveys uncertainty.
- Overly strong handshakes convey pushiness and a disregard to the physical impact of the other party.

Eye contact

When shaking hands, greeting a person for the first time or holding a conversation, be sure to make (and hold) eye contact with the other individual. Make sure you blink; some people unintentionally stare without blinking at the other individual, creating an intimidating and uncomfortable situation.

Arm length space

As a sign of respect to various cultures and individuals, it is important to give each person their personal space. As a rule of thumb, stand a full arm distance between you and the other individual in your conversation. This is especially important when speaking with members of the opposite sex.

Posture

- Your posture speaks to your self-esteem.
- Your back should be straight, shoulders squared, and head up.
- To improve your posture, pretend there is a string at the very top of your head. Pull the string straight up until your shoulders straighten to improve your stance and sitting posture.

Chewing gum

Never chew gum during an interview or anywhere in the proximity of the interview.

Eating

Brush up on dining etiquette if you are participating in an interview or meeting over a meal. Never chew or speak with your mouth full.

Do not order spaghetti during a meal meeting; the long noodles are likely to splash the red sauce onto your clothing.

CHARISMA

Charisma is primarily driven from self-esteem, comfort in yourself, and an empathy for others, all wrapped with flair of finesse and confidence. Charisma is noted by the ability to effortlessly lead people without having any authority over them. Individuals with the gift of Leading and Pastoring generally possess some level of charisma.

This attribute became essential for leaders because the magnetism of charisma creates a natural following that is important for moving an organization forward. There are three recommendations for improving charisma.

1. Listening carefully to what matters to the other person, then linking your topics and examples to helping their concerns.
2. Modeling and charm classes: these types of classes teach you how to walk, stand, sit, and enter a room in a way that almost demands attention.
3. Personal Speaking Coach
   - Align your facial expressions with your message
   - Get comfortable and communicate with confidence
   - Get to know the people you are speaking to. You can diminish the gap between you and your target audience by learning about them and their situations. Then link the information you have discovered about them to your topic.

STRENGTHENING YOUR CHARACTER

THE CHARACTER ELEMENT ANSWERS THE QUESTION, HOW DO YOU FIT INTO THE COMPANY'S CULTURE?

People who are really creative and love change are typically strong in the Character element. This is the third of the four elements. This brand element is typically observed once a job is obtained. This element becomes more pronounced if your Expertise and Impact elements are low and as a result, has a tremendous impact on performance reviews and your ability to be promoted. These are the attributes they look into to explain either the lack of Impact or why there is such high Impact.

Image
Attributes
1. Adapting to change 2. Personal learning development 3. Ownership 4. Integrity and trust 5. Dependability

ADAPTING TO CHANGE

The past decade has encompassed three global shifts that have had life-changing impact to employment as we knew it.

1. **2006 – 2008 Financial Crisis:** The crash of the mortgage, bank, and auto industries forced companies to downsize to stay afloat. The trickledown effect created one of the highest unemployment rates this country has seen since the Great Depression. This also created new regulations which meant companies must learn how to operate significantly differently than in the past. Companies are facing the grim reality of how to do more with less people in order to maintain similar profit margins.
2. **Increase in sophisticated Information Technology:** While the first smart phone was created in 1992, it was not adopted by the masses until Apple launched the infamous iPhone in 2007. That has since changed the face of communications as we know it. In less than a decade, the smart phones, pads and tablets have taken over. Communication is sent and received in seconds. All generations, nations, and demographical groups have adopted using high-end technology for instant information.
3. **Viral adoption of social media:** The use of social media has spread like wild fire. eBizMBA monitors the most frequently visited sites on a daily basis. The list of the 15 most popular sites is found in the marketing chapter of this book.

The use of social media began as a completely personal tool for individuals to link together and share. However, companies have recognized this as a prime vehicle for doing business, and therefore are identifying methods for using these tools to expand their business. Interesting enough, while companies are adopting the use of these types of sites, terminations linked to the personal use of social media during work hours has become so significant that prohibiting the use of them during work hours has become part of companies' employment policies.

So what does all this mean? It means change (and in many cases, FAST and FREQUENT change) is a part of most companies' culture. Companies must stay flexible when it comes to both technology and processes to meet the expectations of very savvy consumers.

The Adapting to Change attribute is important to demonstrate your value to hiring managers. Being an expert in this attribute communicates to them how you can be an asset to moving their company forward instead of a barrier that keeps them stagnant.

Many people struggle with adapting to change either because the complexity of advancing technology is too difficult to comprehend or because of fear of failure. More easily stated, there is comfort in familiarity and discomfort in the unknown.

OVERCOMING TECHNOLOGY

Sometimes what we need to overcome a challenge or mental block is a paradigm shift. Most employers are willing to train on technology changes. One thing to keep in mind is the more you learn, the more marketable you become. Each new system and new process makes YOU more valuable. So instead of becoming frustrated with the new system, become appreciative of the company helping you to become more industry-valuable.

IDENTIFYING AND ADDRESSING FEAR

Another common barrier to change is FEAR. There are three that are consistently present in career matters.

- Fear of Failure
- Fear of Being Unneeded
- Fear of the Unknown
- Fear of Rejection

When fear is the barrier, identify alternative myth busters.

Myth	Truth
Fear of Being Unneeded	When you learn something new, it makes you more valuable not less. Not staying current is actually far more risky than staying stagnant.
Fear of Failure	Failing is part of learning. In many cases we learn more and become more astute from having to try something more than once. Not learning something the first time does not mean we cannot learn it at all. However, if we never try, we most certainly will never learn. So, failure becomes a self-fulfilling prophecy not because you were not capable, but rather because you were unwilling.
Fear of The Unknown	No one knows everything. But two things are typically true: if you think you can, you are correct; and if you think you cannot, you are also correct. The moral of the story is, do not allow negative thinking to become a selffulfilling prophecy.
Fear of Rejection	Through rejection we learn, refine, and strengthen ourselves, and sometimes dodge the unforeseen bullet.
Write Your Own	

SELF DEVELOPMENT

To demonstrate value, it helps to constantly evolve and adapt. Here are a few tips:

- Create a list of professional knowledge, skills, and/or abilities to enhance each year.
- Seek out well-respected individuals to learn from.
- Work with your existing manager to discuss the plan and how to fit in what you've learned to enhance the business.
- Volunteer to do a stretch assignment or learn a new function.

OWNERSHIP

The opposite of ownership is those who live based on the "Entitlement Syndrome." These self-absorbed individuals are like nails on a chalk board. Their behavior becomes an instant and lingering irritant. They are known to only focus on their single part of the big picture. This person will let the entire project or company fail (even if they could have helped stopped it) and be the first to say what was not their role or that no one told them to do something.

Personal ownership is about taking control of your responsibilities and the big picture. Individuals who are strong in personal ownership have a mind-set of accountability. They work diligently to ensure whatever they touch is completed on time and properly.

A person who demonstrates ownership is allergic to the words "That is not my job." His or her focus is on how to make it work.

INTEGRITY AND TRUST

INTEGRITY

A person with high integrity is a person who is viewed as consistently upholding or adhering to moral and ethical principles, such as honesty.

Stephen M. R. Covey writes, "Integrity includes but goes beyond honesty. Honesty is telling the truth—in other words, conforming our words to reality. Integrity is conforming reality to our words—in other words, keeping promises and fulfilling expectations."

TRUST

One fantastic resource on building trust is Stephen M. R. Covey's book, *"The Speed of Trust."* In it he made a profound statement regarding relationships and managing through conflict. Stephen explains that a key component to conflict between people is their lack of trust in themselves and others. Covey defines trust as having confidence in the other individual, in either their character or their competence. Distrust means suspension of the other individuals in either their character or confidence. It's very possible to be trusted in one area and not the other.

He then ask two profound questions. First, who do you trust? Second, who trusts you?

When you think of personal and professional relationships, how would individuals respond if asked about the trust level they have in you? Then ask yourself what behaviors you demonstrate that build or distract from trust.

DEPENDABILITY

The last attribute of the Character element is dependability. Dependability means being able to be counted on. To enhance this attribute focus on:

1. Understanding how your contributions impact the big picture
2. Ensure you do your part every time, all the time, and on time
3. To achieve the "Expert" level in this attribute you must OVER deliver.
4. Last but not least, DO what you say you will do.

Helpful Hints

- If you are listed as an Expert under Impact, one helpful hint for dependability is to learn to say no. Frequently this individual over-commits and therefore under-delivers. Learning the two-letter word "no" can prove extremely helpful in strengthening this attribute.

- However, if you are not an Expert under Impact, then saying NO may not be a good solution for you in this instance. It may be that you need assistance with learning prioritization and time-management techniques.

LATRICE COLLINS

STRENGTHENING YOUR IMPACT

THE IMPACT ELEMENT ANSWERS THE QUESTION, WHAT WILL YOU DO FOR THE ORGANIZATION?

All talk but no action! That is the LAST description you ever want linked to your brand. Millions of hardworking people are dedicated to their jobs. Yet there seems to be a disconnect between what they see as their performance and how they are seen by the person in charge.

If you want to ignite your Impact element, dive into this chapter ASAP and begin creating measureable and noticeable results.

Impact
Attributes
1. Drive and perseverance 2. Customer impact/ added value 3. Compliance 4. Productivity 5. Judgment

DRIVE AND PERSERVERANCE

The slogan for this attribute is "make it happen." There is nothing quite as valuable as having an employee who makes things happen. It relieves so much pressure from a manager when they do not have to resolve every crisis or fix every problem.

Employees with drive help companies grow. They help move beyond problems. They make the manager's job easier. Here are a few affirmations that will help others see you as driven:

- When something does not work, think, "How can I fix it?"
- If there is a barrier that is preventing progress, think, "How can I move it, go over it, around it, or through it?"
- If there is no clear solution, think, "What is an alternative solution?"

Here is a huge tip: If you use the word "try" or "trying," stop immediately. When the word is said, it creates a negative image of you in the other person's mind.

When you say, "I will try," the manager hears, "I will make a lame attempt, but there is a good chance I probably will not make it happen, so do not depend on me."

Instead, make sure you understand the scope of what the manager is asking and state, "I will work to make this happen or provide you with alternative solutions." This will let the manager know you can be counted on to move the business forward.

CUSTOMER IMPACT/ADDED VALUE

Have you ever frequented a particular restaurant because you loved the atmosphere and the people more than the food? Do you have an expectation of service when you speak to the concierge at a hotel? Have you ever rated a company higher (or lower) because of how they looked out for you instead of their actual product?

Every interaction with a company is an experience that leaves an impression.

Customer impact and added value reflects how the customer feels and the lasting impact you made with him or her after they have left your acquaintance.

There is a customer service training class called the Fred Factor. It is about how an average person (Fred the mailman) provided extraordinary service like getting to know the people on his route, placing packages in discreet areas to ensure no harm came to them, and looking out for the mail needs of the people he serviced.

Fred received constant praise and reviews for doing what he considered basic services that others saw as extraordinary. This is different than service quality, which links to the interaction. Customer Impact links to the added value you had to the customer.

Make a list of what you can do to provide an extra level of impact to your internal or external customers.

Examples can be simple but might be very meaningful to other individuals, like giving a client a heads-up or a reminder call, or remembering something that was important to them, like a child's first dance. It could be staying a little later to help them or coming in earlier to help. Simple behaviors add huge impact to the customer and links back to your brand image.

COMPLIANCE

You might ask, why is compliance under the Impact element? It is because this attribute helps minimize risk and liability to the company. Companies create policies and guidelines to help improve efficiencies and minimize risk and/or liability.

Individuals who are constantly pushing the envelope of compliance represent higher risk to the organization. Therefore, it is important to follow the company's established guidelines.

However, if the guideline is faulty (meaning, not costeffective or it increases rather than decreases risks to the organization) then it is good to recommend a valid alternative that could help the company.

If you are recommending a change to a company's policy it would be received better if you link your recommendation to at least one of the following:

- Cost Savings (Efficiencies)
- Decreased Risk
- Decreased Liability

- Improved Customer Satisfaction
- Improve Profit

PRODUCTIVITY

This is truly the bottom line. When a person thinks of you, how do they answer the question, "What do you do for the company?"

It does not matter what industry you work in or what type of role you are in, you MUST be able to quantitatively prove you can produce!

So how do you do this?

First, identify what the organization uses to measure their star performer. Here are a few examples:
- Number of Items Sold
- Number of Calls Made
- Number of Accounts Collected
- Projects Completed on Time
- Amount of Money Saved
- Quality Score Results
- Customer Service Survey Results
- Percentage of Work Completion Within Time Frame
- Accuracy With Cash
- Number of Projects Implemented

When communicating your production impact for a company, summarize your accomplishments by looking at the impact across larger periods of time (such as by quarter, year, or over five years). For instance:

- Maintaining a 98 percent quality score rating over two years sounds a great deal stronger than over one month, or
- Saved the company $120,000 over one year sounds better than $2,500 one week.

JUDGEMENT

Poor judgement is typically a symbol of not considering all the critical facts and who (or what) the decision impacts. The following five questions are proven to be helpful in improving judgment:

1. Are you the expert of the issue at hand? If not, who do I need to get involved to help make the decision?
2. Who else is impacted? If the decision impacts others, then involve others to determine how the decision will touch other areas.
3. Do the facts support the decision? In other words, do the facts say the decision should help or harm the organization?
4. Is this the right time? Is something else happening that will impact the decision or that the decision impacts?
5. What are the pros and cons of the decision? Consider the impact to the company, the customers (internal or external), your peers, your employees, and yourself.

Sound judgement comes from gathering facts and making the best possible decision for all people involved.

MARKETING YOUR BRAND

MARKETING YOUR BRAND

Marketing is the comprehensive strategy that focuses on reinforcing the image you want others to have of your brand.

When companies market their brand, they think about all their "touch points," and how to strengthen their brand image through each one.

For companies, a touch point represents every time the customer is exposed to the company. Examples of touch points include telephone interactions, letters (or written material to customers), commercials, advertisement, community involvement, and/or web presence.

Marketing your Perfect Fit brand is similar to marketing a company. Just like with companies, there are a variety of touch points to communicate your brand. There are two different categories of touch points for your personal career brand:

1. written representation
2. personal representation

WRITTEN REPRESENTATION

Written representation encompasses marketing pieces that introduce you to others. The typical three for job seekers are resumes, cover letters, and social media platforms. Remember that the purpose of marketing is to create interest that will entice companies to contact you for an interview.

THE BASICS TOOLS

- Cover letter: a cover letter is a narrative introduction of you. It typically accompanies the resume. If you plan to use a cover letter, it is recommended to use a "Tstyle," and make sure to keep your information short and concise. The Internet provides free samples of this type of cover letter format.

  It is also helpful to use the words from the job posting that directly apply to your experience into the cover letter. This will help your cover letter and experience stand out.

- There are two types of resumes.
  - Chronological: this type of resume provides a listing of work-related experience in date order. It is organized with the most recent job first.
  - Functional: this resume organizes the experience based on functions (such as sales, marketing, construction work) instead of chronological. This is a great option for individuals new to the workforce or those interested in changing careers.

INTERNET MARKETING TOOLS

This is the day of instant information. If someone wants to learn more about you, they can simply type your name into the Internet and voila, the hiring manager can see text, images, messages, and virtually anything open for the public to see.

Social media has exploded as a form of getting to know potential employees. A few well-used social media sites include LinkedIn, Facebook, and Twitter.

To tailor how you would like others to see you, there are steps you can take to shape your image and market yourself successfully.

PERSONAL WEBSITE

Creating your personal Web site allows you to present the image you want others to see. You can include your experience, accomplishments, pictures (if you like), etc. What is great is you can do it for free. You can also use it to post work samples and/or references.

Various online sites are available that allow you to create individual websites at little or no cost. To find free website tools, type the words "free websites" in the Internet search box.

PERSONAL REPRESENTATION

It is a fatal error to believe your brand is only showcased through your written marketing tools. There are multiple touch points to showcase your brand. The personal representation includes the impression you make with others through interviewing and networking with friends, family, peers, or managers.

Two charts have been provided to cross-reference opportunities to market each brand attribute.

Additional information is available throughout this book to strengthen the various brand touch points.

VOLUNTEERING YOUR BRAND STRENGTHS

A third method of marketing your brand is through volunteerism. This is especially helpful if you need to repair your brand or showcase the strength of your brand.

Volunteering to assist others in need speaks to your character and your skills. This is also a way of keeping your skills sharpened.

The more you voluntarily help others, the more free publicity you have on who you are and what you can do for others. This simple task is often cited as how people obtain referrals and recommendations for jobs openings.

Remember the old saying, "It is not what you know, but who you know"? Well, in reality it is about who knows you, and what they think of you.

LATRICE COLLINS

BRAND APPLICATION MATRIX

BRAND MARKETING STRATEGIC TOUCH POINTS
Written representation

Brand Elements/Attributes	Written Representation				
	Cover Letter	Resume	Emails	Social Media	Personal Websites
EXPERTISE					
Job Knowledge	●	●		◉	●
Business Knowledge	●	●			●
Work Quality	◉	◉	●		●
Teachability					
Credibility	●	●		◉	●
IMAGE					
Interpersonal Skills		◉	●		◉
Service Quality	◉	◉			◉
Verbal Skills					
Appearance					
Charisma		◉			◉
CHARACTER					
Adapting to Change	●	●	●		
Personal Dev. & Learning		◉			
Ownership					
Integrity & Trust					
Dependability					
IMPACT					
Drive & Perseverance	●	◉			◉
Customer Impact	●	●		●	◉
Compliance					
Productivity	●	●			◉
Judgement			●	●	

BRAND MARKETING STRATEGIC TOUCH POINTS
Personal representation

Brand Elements/Attributes	Personal Representation				
	Interviews	Networking Event	Presenting to Groups	Peers & Manager	Friends & Family
EXPERTISE					
Job Knowledge	●	●	●	●	◉
Business Knowledge	●	●	●	●	◉
Work Quality	◉	●		●	◉
Teachability	●	◉		●	●
Credibility	●	●	●	●	●
IMAGE					
Interpersonal Skills	●	●	●	●	●
Service Quality	●	●	●	●	●
Verbal Skills	●	●	●	●	●
Appearance	●	●	●	●	●
Charisma	●	●	●	●	●
CHARACTER					
Adapting to Change	●	●		●	●
Personal Dev. & Learning		●		●	
Ownership			●	●	●
Integrity & Trust		●		●	●
Dependability		●		●	●
IMPACT					
Drive & Perseverance	●	●	●	●	◉
Customer Impact	●	◉	●	●	
Compliance	●			●	
Productivity	●	◉		●	
Judgement	●	●		●	◉

LATRICE COLLINS

WHAT YOU NEED AND WANT

Now that you have taken time to discover more about you, the next step is to figure out what you are looking for from a company. Ask yourself what type of company you want to work for. This can be a really challenging question for people who have a diverse career. So let us start with the big picture and work down.

First, what type of industry would you like to work in? While this may at first seem just as difficult, it will become apparent that you are not comfortable with just any industry. Use the next few pages to check off the types of industries you can see yourself happily driving to work in every day.

ATMOSPHERE FOR GREATEST POTENTIAL (AGP)

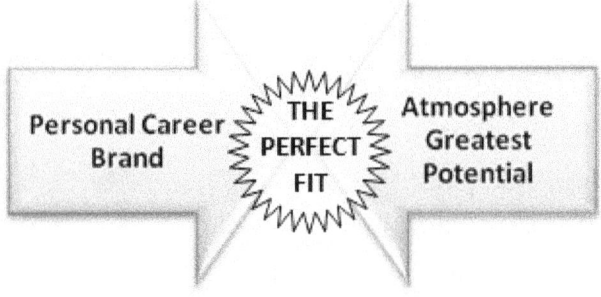

Now that you have worked through your personal brand, let us dive into the AGP (Atmosphere of Greatest Potential).

When considering a company and/or position, complete the AGP pyramid to identify if the company is a fit for you based on the criteria you have identified in the "What You Want and Need" section.

INDUSTRY

(Check your industry preferences)

- ☐ Accounting and auditing services
- ☐ Advertising and PR services
- ☐ Aerospace and defense
- ☐ Advertising and PR services
- ☐ Aerospace and defense
- ☐ Agriculture/forestry/fishing
- ☐ Architectural and design services
- ☐ Automotive and parts manufacturing
- ☐ Automotive sales and repair services
- ☐ Biotechnology/pharmaceuticals
- ☐ Broadcasting, music, and film
- ☐ Business services—Other
- ☐ Chemicals/petrochemicals
- ☐ Clothing and textile manufacturing
- ☐ Computer hardware
- ☐ Computer software
- ☐ Computer/IT services
- ☐ Construction—industrial facilities and infrastructure
- ☐ Construction—residential and commercial/office
- ☐ Consumer packaged goods manufacturing
- ☐ Education

- ☐ Electronics, components, and semiconductor manufacturing.
- ☐ Energy and utilities
- ☐ Engineering services
- ☐ Entertainment venues and theaters
- ☐ Financial services and banking
- ☐ Food and beverage production
- ☐ Government and military
- ☐ Healthcare services
- ☐ Hotels and lodging
- ☐ Insurance
- ☐ Internet services
- ☐ Legal services
- ☐ Management consulting services
- ☐ Manufacturing—others
- ☐ Marine manufacturing and services
- ☐ Medical devices and supplies
- ☐ Metals and minerals
- ☐ Nonprofit charitable organizations
- ☐ Other/not classified
- ☐ Performing and fine arts
- ☐ Personal and household services
- ☐ Printing and publishing
- ☐ Real estate/property management

- ☐ Rental services
- ☐ Restaurant/food services
- ☐ Retail
- ☐ Security and surveillance
- ☐ Sports and physical recreation
- ☐ Staffing/employment agencies
- ☐ Telecommunications services
- ☐ Transport and storage—materials
- ☐ Travel, transportation, and tourism
- ☐ Waste management
- ☐ Wholesale trade/import-export

Once you have narrowed your scope by finding an industry, let us look at the type of company structure and culture that is more appealing to you.

AGP PYRAMID

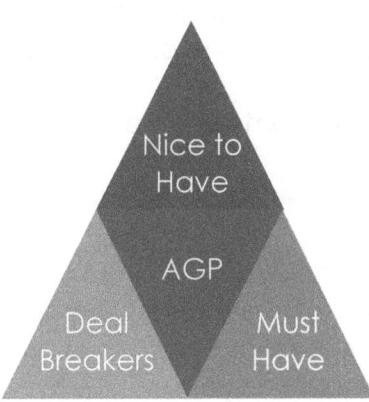

Before you begin any job search, take the time to identify what you need and want from the organization. The relationship between you and your employer goes two ways. Since the average person spends more time at work than anything else, it is important to enjoy the company you work for.

The purpose of the AGP section is to identify the type of atmosphere that best fulfills your personal needs at this point in your life.

The remaining pages in this section list characteristics found in a company. As you review each item, mark each with one of the following letters.

      M = Must be present
      N = Nice to have, but not required
      D = Deal breaker
           (This characteristic SHOULD NOT be present)

If none of the three descriptors listed above applies, leave it blank. If we missed something that is important to you, write it into the blank provided at the end of each list.

Let us begin with the company's overall structure.

Company size:

___ Less than 500 employees
___ More than 500 but less than 5000 employees
___ More than 5000 employees
___ National or global presence

___ _____

Work environment
___ Union environment
___ Nonunion environment
___ Call center environment
___ Plant environment
___ Office environment
___ Higher-education environment
     (such as an IT or financially focused environment)
___ Results driven
___ Flexible workflow
___ Repetitive workflow

___ _____

Facility attributes
___ Distance from home (_____ miles or _____ minutes)
___ On-site cafeteria
___ On-site daycare

___ _____

Company focus

___ Profit focused (focus is on shareholders)
___ Community-focused (focus on issues designed to help people)
___ Health-focused (healing or aiding the sick or elderly)
___ Animal-focused (care for animals)
___ Green-focused (save the planet)
___ _____

Benefit packages

___ Medical, dental, vision
___ Life insurance, short- and long-term disability plans
___ Retirement plans
___ 401k options
___ Time off from work (vacation, holiday, and sick)
___ _____

Compensation package

___ Signing bonus
___ Straight base pay (no commission)
___ Commission pay
___ Bonuses
___ Severance package
___ Volunteer day
___ _____

COMPANY CULTURE AND CHARACTER

Culture

Since companies are run by people, each company has its own culture and character. The culture of a company describes the atmosphere and norms shared by the people within the organization. Sometimes this is clearly stated, and other times it is more subtle. Questions to ask yourself about the company culture include:

- What are their stated values or principles?
- How do they treat their employees?
- What do they do for the community?

Character

You might ask why character is important. It only requires a thirty-second reflection of the state of our economy to realize the extreme impact of companies that operate without reasonable character.

Companies strong on character invest in both their employees and their communities. The health of the world is like a recycling process. As companies grow from consumers, they give back by developing their employees and supporting their community through time, money, or both. As individuals grow, they buy products or services from the companies.

We have listed eight key areas to help identify the character of a company. The answer to the character test is based on your perspective of how the company stacks up to the character questions.

Note: Many of these questions will be answered either through your research or during the various interactions with the company.

Life balance

___ Family-oriented
___ Work-from-home option
___ Career-focused
___ Flexible hours

___ _____

Dress code

___ Professional (suit and tie)
___ Business casual (khakis, golf shirts, etc.)
___ Casual (jeans)

___ _____

Atmosphere

___ Corporate
___ Highly structured
___ Military
___ Lighthearted
___ Team environment is encouraged
___ Formal training is provided
___ Leadership development training is provided

___ _____

Diversity

Diversity is defined as a body of people who represent clearly distinctive and versatile mindsets. This could include different races, age, genders, family status, educational background, cultures, etc.
___ Diversity is present
___ Diversity is valued
___ Equal opportunity for promotion for all is present
___ Corporate-sponsored network groups and functions
___ _____

Management style

___ Autonomous work environment
   (i.e., tell me what to do and let me do it)
___ Hands-on collaboration with manager
___ Open-door policy
___ Enforce the chain of command
___ Individual reward and recognition
___ Employees are valued
___ Flexible workflow
___ Repetitive workflow
___ Rewards of loyalty
___ Rewards based on hard work and results

ROLES

List what type of roles you are interested in. For instance, would you like to be a personal assistant or an operations manager?

Specific roles

Specific activities

Sometimes you are not sure what specific role you like, but you know the types of activities you enjoy. Take a moment to list work related activities you enjoy doing that you are also GOOD at doing.

It is important that you identify these items BEFORE you begin your interviewing process. This will ensure you do not waste your time and that you do not accept a position that will make you miserable in the not-too-distant future.

So now let us take the time to organize all the ratings you have given each part of what you need and want from a company. This will give you one list of reference when considering the company(ies) that will represent your atmosphere of greatest potential.

Nice to Have

Deal Breaker

Must Have

NETWORKING

There are often misconceptions regarding networking. Some people see networking as simply attending a large meeting where you pass out business cards to complete strangers. Other times it is viewed as an opportunity to meet influential people who can do something for you. Well, let me give you a clue: BOTH of these perspectives are INEFFECTIVE means of networking.

Effective networking involves creating a two-way relationship. Strong networking relationships involve two or more people with mutual interests who like and respect each other. One of the best approaches to networking is to first seek to understand the person and THEIR needs, then identify if there is a way you can help them. The help you provide can strengthen the relationship and create a lasting impression of you to the other party.

There is myth that says networking is based on who you know. On the contrary, networking is about who knows you and WHAT they think of you. Try this exercise: When meeting a new person (especially one at a networking event), listen closely to them. Find out their immediate struggles and needs. Next, identify if there is a way you can help that person, whether it is something you can do directly or something someone you know can possibly help them with. Offer solutions (short or long term) to help meet the person's needs and offer them one or more "no strings attached" solutions.

> *Warning! Make sure you balance how much volunteer time you offer. When you have determined you have done enough to demonstrate your strengths, feel free to offer additional services for a fee.*

The good news is, typically once you open yourself to helping others, your brand reputation precedes you and offers you more opportunities than the old way of networking.

Your first order of business is to create a relationship where you and the other individual(s) can identify what you have in common and how you can possibly help each other.

TIPS TO NETWORKING

- Approach each encounter as a chance to meet a great person whom maybe you can help with a solution for their problem. This is done at no charge for no reward; maybe there is an immediate job lead or maybe not. The point is to develop a meaningful relationship by which you can help a friend – and just maybe, they know a friend who can use someone like you.

- Take business cards to every function. If you are not working, have some created at the neighborhood office supply store, at home, or through Vistaprint for usually under $25. Make sure you include your name, phone number, email address and your profession.

- If you forget names, make a point of using the person's name in a sentence three times. This will help you remember.

- Be sincere.

- Make eye contact and give a strong handshake.

- Write notes on the back of business cards regarding where you met the individual and something about your conversation so it will help you both remember each other later.

- Place cards you receive from people you want to follow up with in a different pocket than those you do not; this will help ensure you focus the right attention on the right cards later.

- Find a reason to follow up with the person after the event.

- Follow up with the stack of cards you are interested in within three days of the event so you can be fresh in their minds.

- Stay pleasant and optimistic at all times if possible; remember your aura.

DON'TS OF NETWORKING

As important as it is to do certain things during networking, it is equally important to avoid doing some things when you network. Here is a helpful list of networking don'ts.

- Do not be overly demanding of their time.
- Do not forget to follow up.
- Do not be late for your appointments.
- Do not take advantage of their time.
- Do not say someone referred you if he or she did not.
- Do not hog the conversation.

- Do not forget to bring something to write with and on.
- Do not forget to say their name at least three times to remember it. The worst thing you can do is continue to call a person the WRONG name.

FINDING LEADS

You have:

- identified your brand image,
- determined strategies for enhancing your brand,
- identified the atmosphere for greatest potential, and
- discovered the dos and don'ts of networking

Now you are ready to begin to seek out leads for potential job openings.

Leads to jobs can be found absolutely anywhere. The days of expecting jobs to be found in the newspaper are antiquated. Most jobs are found on the Internet, but even more are simply not posted and found primarily through word-of-mouth.

Here are a few options to help you brainstorm where to find leads.

ONLINE

- 100kjob.com
- careerbuilders.com
- hotjobs.yahoo.com
- hundredk.com
- indeed.com
- jobs.com
- monster.com
- perfectlocaljobs.com
- snagajob.com
- simplyhired.com
- sixfigure.com
- theladders.com

ASSOCIATIONS

- Trade associations
- Associations based on hobbies
- Associations based on religion
- Educational events
- Fraternities
- Sororities
- Speaker groups
- Toastmasters special interest groups

COMMUNITY EVENTS

- Fairs
- Volunteer clubs
- PTA meetings
- Home-owner association meetings
- Job fairs
- Church functions
- Chamber of commerce meetings
- Small business meetings
- School board meetings
- Grocery stores
- Malls
- _____
- _____
- _____
- _____

LATRICE COLLINS

WINNING THE INTERVIEW

TYPES OF INTERVIEWS

It worked! Someone has called you back and requested you to come in for an interview. There are various types of interviews. Each has its own functionality. so let us learn about each style and its purpose.

1: SCREENING INTERVIEW

A screening interview is typically conducted by human resources and is meant to weed out unqualified candidates.

2: TELEPHONE INTERVIEW

This interview is conducted over the phone. It may be a screening interview, skills assessment, or personality fit interview. If possible, find out the objective of the phone interview and the role of the person who will be conducting the interview before the call.

3: BEHAVIORAL (OR SITUATIONAL) INTERVIEW

Behavioral interviews ask interviewees questions regarding specific events in the past. The purpose is to identify behaviors used in the past, to forecast potential future behavior.

The questions typically start with the words "Tell me about a time..." and are followed up with probing questions such as:

- "What did you do?"
- "Who was involved?"
- "How did it end?"

It is important to be specific in this type of interview and explain exactly what happened. Stay away from general statements such as "usually."

Review your resume the day before an interview. Identify situations that demonstrate your strengths and your brand. For example, recall a situation when you led a team, managed a project, or handled a very difficult customer. How did you resolve each situation? Have these types of items in mind for when the interviewer ask you behavior types of interview questions.

4: GROUP INTERVIEW

Two or more individuals interview you at one time. Oftentimes this is done to save time. It also allows the group to discuss the candidate as a whole when the interview is over.

Make sure that during a group interview, you make eye contact with each interviewer throughout the meeting. Focusing only on one person can offend the others and distract them from you discussing your qualifications.

5: INFORMATIONAL INTERVIEW

An informational interview is usually requested by a candidate to seek out information and guidance. In this case, the candidate becomes the interviewer.

This type of interview is generally requested to gain insight ranging from understanding the industry to education requirements and unwritten competencies.

This is a great type of interview for getting your foot in the door and making an excellent first impression.

6: ONE-ON-ONE INTERVIEW

One-on-one interviews have a wide range of objectives. Some are designed to test your knowledge and skills, while others are designed to determine if you are a fit for the company. Note that dozens of people may qualify for a position, but only a few would fit into the culture of the company.

When possible, find out from the person scheduling all the meetings the objective of each meeting, and obtain a little insight on each interviewer. This information will be priceless.

7: LUNCH INTERVIEW

The lunch interview is similar to the one-on-one interview; however, it takes place at a location away from the company. While this interview is designed to provide a casual and

comfortable atmosphere, make sure you brush up on your dining etiquette skills. Poor eating habits can be costly when it comes to the impression you leave.

8: SKILLS INTERVIEW

A skills interview tests your ability and aptitude to do the job. It can range from basic skills such as organizing a file folder to complex skills such as rebuilding an engine. This interview may be time-consuming. Make sure you clarify what level of detail they are seeking (i.e., extreme detail or overview). Do not make any assumptions.

9: STRESS INTERVIEW

Stress interviews are a deliberate attempt to see how you handle yourself under pressure. The interviewer may keep you waiting. He or she may be sarcastic, argumentative, or condescending.

If at any point you feel yourself becoming aggravated, remember that this is a test to see how well you hold up under pressure.

CREATING AN INTERVIEW STRATEGY

BEFORE THE INTERVIEW

DEVELOP A PERSONAL THEME

Use your personal branding results to create a single message

about you. Emphasize your brand strengths whenever possible. Know your strengths as they apply to various aspects of the role. Keep five or six examples ready that support the essence of who you are.

BE FAMILIAR WITH YOUR RESUME

This may seem strange, but sometimes items are on your resume from a long time ago. Perhaps you had your resume rewritten by a professional, and you are not quite familiar with the lingo he/she used.

Make sure you are extremely familiar with every item on your resume. One suggestion is to have a special copy just for you. Your copy will list examples and accomplishment details next to each role to better prepare you for any interview.

RESEARCH

Research everything you can about the company, the division you are interviewing with and how it relates to the parent company, their product lines, plant closures, acquisitions, etc. Use this information to develop questions for the interviewer.

Many companies ask why you are interested in working for their company; the research provides a great opportunity for you to communicate the behind-the-scenes work you completed.

As part of your research, be sure to obtain the following:

From Human Resources:

- An official job description
- The salary range for the position of interest

If follow-up interviews are scheduled:

- Obtain information on the people doing the interviews.
- Identify the types of interviews that will be conducted.
- If possible, find out what is most important about the role to the next interviewer.

To ensure you do not look pushy, ask for the information above at different states of the process. The job description and salary range can be requested before the first interview. The remaining information would be requested after you have been offered the opportunity for follow-up interviews.

PREPARING YOUR INTERVIEW STRATEGY

1. Review the position information.
   Identify your strengths as they compare to the role.

2. Write notes.
   - On a separate paper, write your notes.
   - Include questions to ask the interviewer.
   - Include a list of your accomplishments and proven skills.

3. There are three objectives to any question:
   - identify experience
   - uncover behaviors
   - assess character

Make sure your examples put you in a positive light under any of the three categories.

4. Rehearse.

   Rehearse how you would answer questions based on which level of interviewing you are in. Remember to keep answers short and precise during the screening level interview, but more detailed during the meeting with the hiring manager.

5. Identify questions to ask before you leave.

INTERVIEW PLANNING

WHAT TO TAKE WITH YOU

- Be sure to take a portfolio or briefcase.
  Women: if you are carrying a briefcase, do not carry a purse—it makes you look bulky.
- Bring at least two workable writing utilities
- Have several unfolded clean, crisp resumes printed on bright white paper.
- Have all your questions inside of your portfolio.

ARRIVAL TIME

Aim to be thirty minutes early for every interview; this allows for traffic problems. If possible, drive to the location the day before to ensure you know how to get there. Make sure you have the name of the interviewer spelled out.

While you may arrive at the building early, do not go to the actual appointment until fifteen minutes before the interview; otherwise, the interviewer may feel rushed to see you.

LOOK THE PART

Make sure your hair, makeup, grooming, and hygiene are immaculate.

DRESS CODE

Dress one level higher than the role you are applying for. The

drive-by the day before can provide the opportunity to see the dress code. Also, make sure you ask the person scheduling the interview about the dress code.

SALARY

Do not discuss salary until you have completed the interview process. If the interviewer persists, ask for the range of the position. If you are comfortable and your desired salary is within the range, inform them that you are confident the two sides will agree to a mutually fair salary.

SETTING THE TONE

Be friendly and knowledgeable, but never arrogant.

THE FIRST INTERVIEW

Begin with friendly small talk; keep it relatively generic. If you notice items in their office such as golf clubs (and you play golf), then it is OK to ask them if they play and engage in a conversation about the sport.

It would also be a good idea to bring up general information you discovered about the company. Remember to know your audience. Discuss with the interviewer only that which would interest the interviewer. For instance, a discussion around the recent trade in China may be beyond the knowledge of the head of recruitment; however, the director of global affairs may be inclined to discuss it in more detail.

The primary focus of the first interview is to demonstrate that

you possess the basic knowledge of the role and that you are qualified and eager for the position.

GETTING TO KNOW THE INTERVIEWERS

As you proceed to follow-up interviews, the questions become much more specific. The hiring team is looking more closely at your personality regarding how you resolve problems and determine solutions.

These interviews focus on your personality AND your skills. As you review your notes for experiences that best describe your accomplishments, think about the leadership and analytical characteristics that were involved in completing various tasks.

Questions for this level of interview should highlight your knowledge and leadership level in the position or industry.

Plan to ask no more than two questions, unless the conversation naturally flows into follow-up questions.

Make sure the interviewer feels comfortable with you and not like he/she is being interrogated. You want to come across as knowledgeable of the role and the industry but not more knowledgeable than the person interviewing you.

WHAT TO LEAVE WITH

Do not leave empty handed.

- Make sure you collect business cards from each interviewer. (The cards will be used for thank-you cards and follow-up questions.)
- Collect answers for your most pressing questions.
- Find out the next steps for you in the process.

AFTER THE INTERVIEW

- Make sure you send a thank-you note. Some people send thank-you emails, but a handwritten note is more personal.
- Use the negotiation section to help close the deal.
- If you do not get the job, thank the interviewers for the opportunity and ask if any of them would be willing to coach you on what you could have done differently.
- Stay positive. You never know which encounters will open future doors.

QUESTIONS YOU MAY BE ASKED

- **Would you describe your ideal career?**
  Focus on the features of the position you are applying for and its potential succession plan. If you discuss a career completely out of line from their position, the interviewer may feel you will leave the position because it is not within the career scope you described.

- **Can you tell me what you know about this company?**
  Use information from your research and prior interviews to describe the company from the big picture to the role in question.

- **What would you do differently if you ran the company?**
  Be very careful here. This is a double-edged question. The interviewer wants to see the leader and visionary in you; however, it is important not to belittle or insult the work the company has done so far.

  Begin to answer this question by complimenting the successes of the company, then discuss one or two items that you would recommend implementing including the projected impact it would have on various components of the company.

- **What would you do if one of our competitors offers you a position?**
  Focus on their company being your company of choice. After researching the industry's best, your desire is to grow with them and not consider a career with the competitors.

- **Why are you leaving your current job?**
  Focus on the company's strengths or the function of the position. Determine how it is in line with either your core values or career path.

- **What salary would you expect for this job?**
  First, make sure you have a salary range for the position. If not, ask for it at this time. Then verbally walk through the thought process.

  If you are at the beginning of the interviewing process, politely explain the salary's range is within the expectation of what you are interested in; however, you require a more in-depth understanding of the role before communicating a figure.

  Make sure all negotiations are presented in writing before the offer is accepted.

- **Why should we select you over the other candidates?**
  Your answer should communicate confidence, but not arrogance. Be sure to describe observations people have made about your overall contributions.

- **Tell me about a situation where you lost your temper.**
  Be careful with this question. Questions surrounding emotions typically resurface the actual emotion during the interview. You do not want to show anger or frustration during an interview. Try to express the situation with just enough detail to illustrate the severity of the problem.

Finally, it is critical to close this type of scenario with how you have learned from the incident. Leave the interviewer with a positive impression of you by providing a follow-up example of how you applied what you learned during a more recent situation.

QUESTIONS YOU CAN ASK THE INTERVIEWER

- Is there anything I may have left out that may be critical to your decision regarding my qualifications or natural fit into the role?
- Have I said anything that may concern you regarding my ability to fulfill the role to your satisfaction?
- What position or positions does this job typically lead to?
- I am always looking for ways to meet and exceed my manager's expectations. Can you tell me what your expectations are for those you consider high achievers?
- What skills are considered most useful for success in the job I am applying for? (Note: If the interviewer describes a skill you have not effectively communicated, request permission to elaborate on your experience that you may not have communicated up until that moment.)
- Benefits are typically discussed by the HR person; ask the recruiter benefits-related questions. Only ask personal benefits-related questions after an offer has been made.

SALARY NEGOTIATION TIPS

You made it! They have offered you the position, and now it is the final step: salary negotiation. Like everything else discussed, negotiation is a strategy that requires gathering information, planning your approach, and considering different alternatives and viewpoints for all parties. It is important to communicate clearly and specifically and make decisions to reach your goal.

Do your homework! Several sites provide average salary for your years of experience in your city, such as salary.com. Before communicating your desired salary, check with the experts to know what is a reasonable request.

Here are ten important negotiation tips to consider:

1. First rule of thumb, do not discuss salary at the beginning of the interview process.
2. Do not provide your salary history until it is time to negotiate salary.
3. Search the Internet for free advice on how to negotiate.
4. Find out from HR what the salary range is for the position.
5. During the interview process, be sure to ask for the three critical strengths the hiring manager feels would be ideal for the role. The more qualified you are, the higher the salary you can request.
6. Once you understand the three critical strengths the manager wants to see, be sure to expound on your experience as it relates to each item (do this in a confident yet NOT boastful manner).

7. Consider your experience level. Depending on how high you are in those strengths, your proven track record helps determine where you should fall on the range of the scale. Beyond what you have done in the past, consider how much you can provide to the company's future.
8. Consider your experience level; depending on how high you are in those strengths, your proven track record helps determine where you should fall on the range of the scale. Beyond what you have done in the past, consider how much you can provide to the company's future.
9. Develop a list of what you would like from the employer (base pay, bonus, signing bonus, vacation time, flex work hours, benefits, etc.). Identify what is critical and what is negotiable. BE REASONABLE, using a win-win mind-set. Remember this is a two-way relationship.
10. ASK for it. Listen closely to the response. A "no" may be a "not now" or "maybe." If so, renegotiate your desired salary based on their statement. For example, if they state they cannot pay a certain amount now, see if they would consider an increase of a certain amount at your three-month or six-month anniversary.
11. Get all offers in writing!

Congratulations!

You have successfully completed *The Career Brand™ for Professionals*. We hope you have learned more about your personal career brand and are empowered to conduct a successful job search.

We would love to hear your success stories. Please feel free to email us at info@TheCareerBrand.com so we can share your success with others.

ABOUT THE AUTHOR

Latrice Collins has lived every day of her life to fulfill her purpose of inspiring change. Today, her career has encompassed multiple levels of accomplishments.

Her background includes the following roles:

- Television talk show host
- An executive at multiple Fortune 500 companies
- Adjunct professor of strategic planning and managerial marketing
- Author, orator, and national motivational speaker
- Executive coach
- Toastmasters club president and district contest winner

Collins cares about helping others and focuses on developing individuals and organizations with a passion for growth. She holds an undergraduate degree in business management from the University of Illinois at Chicago and an executive MBA from New York Institute of Technology, where she graduated with high honors. Collins currently resides in the Dallas, Texas, area.

www.ingramcontent.com/pod-product-compliance
Lightning Source LLC
Chambersburg PA
CBHW061654040426
42446CB00010B/1727